WOLF

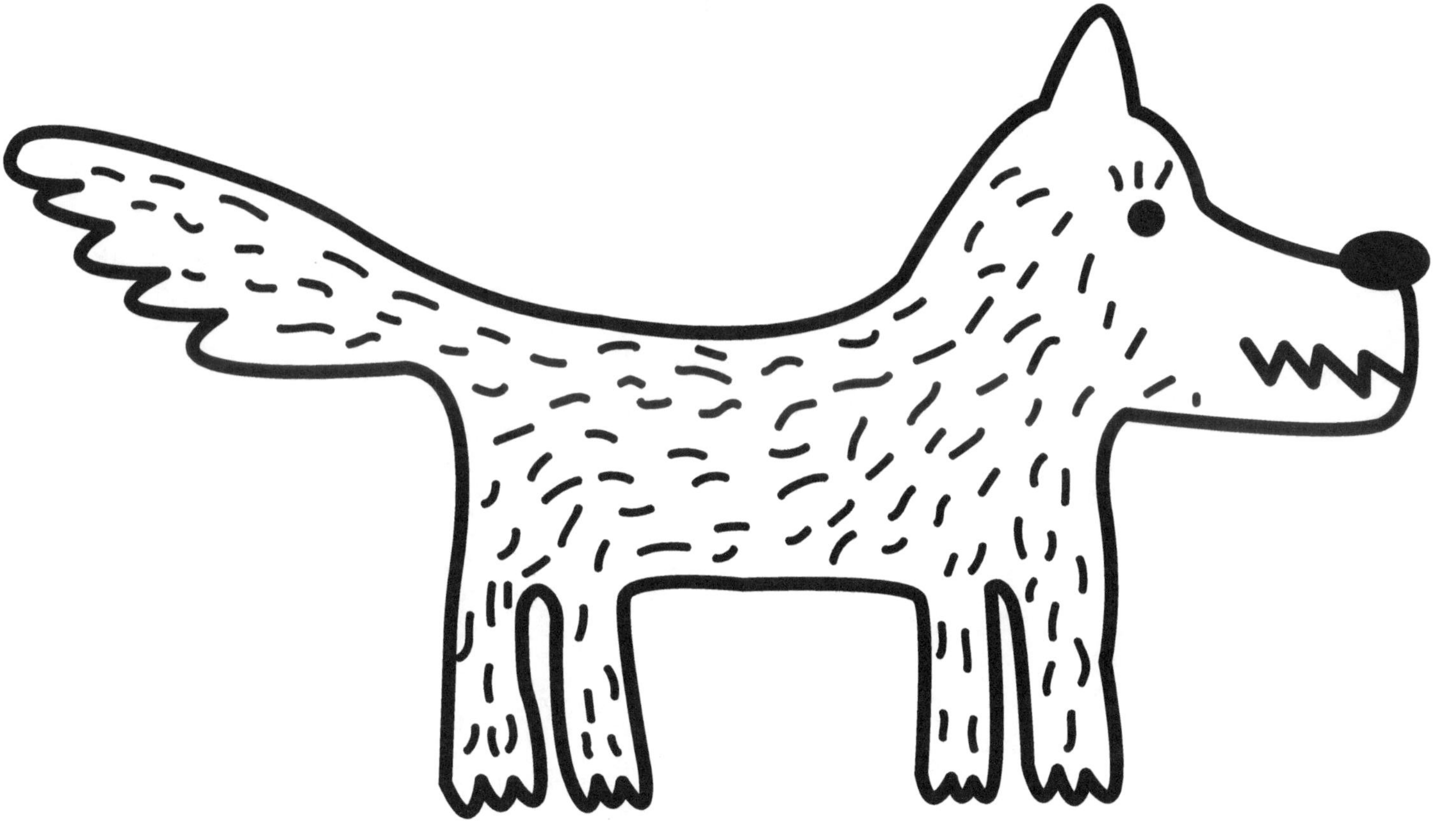

SHARK

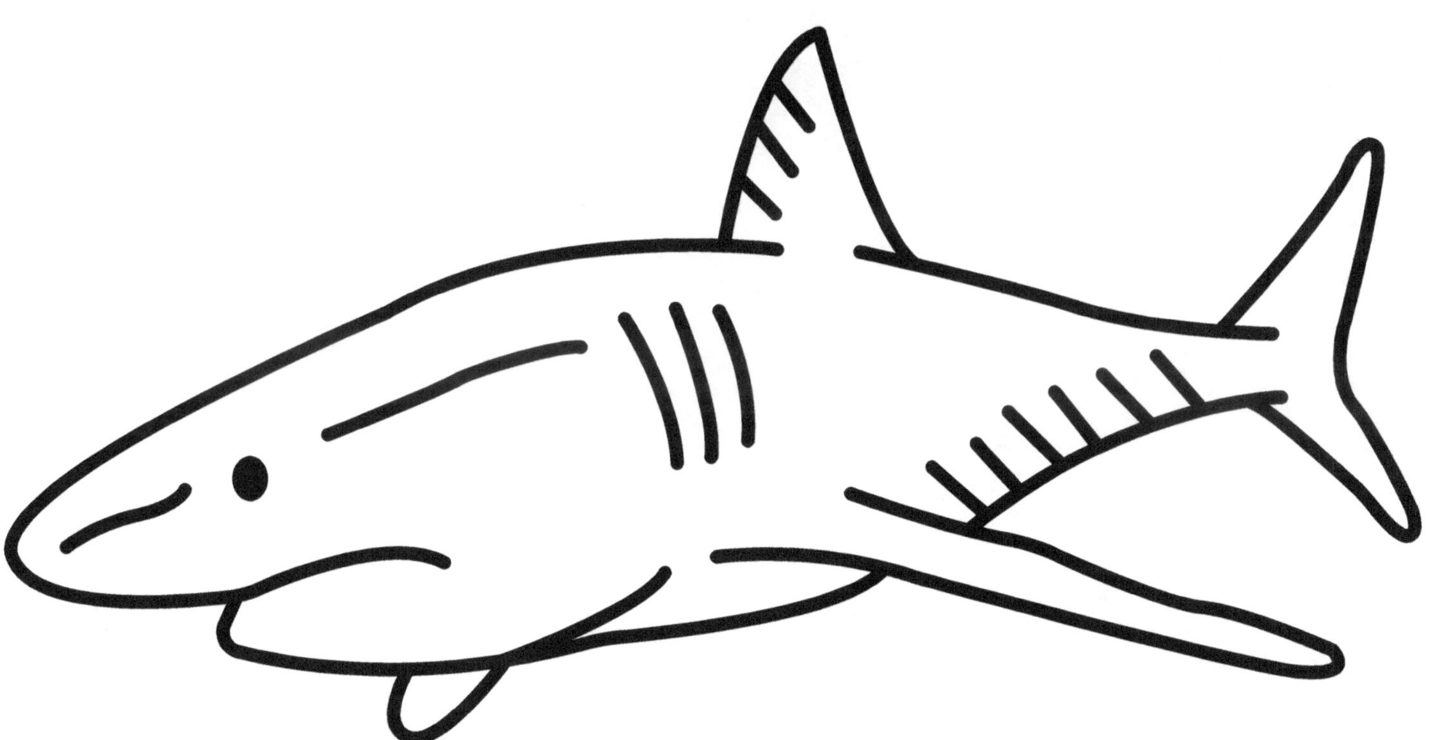

MONKEY

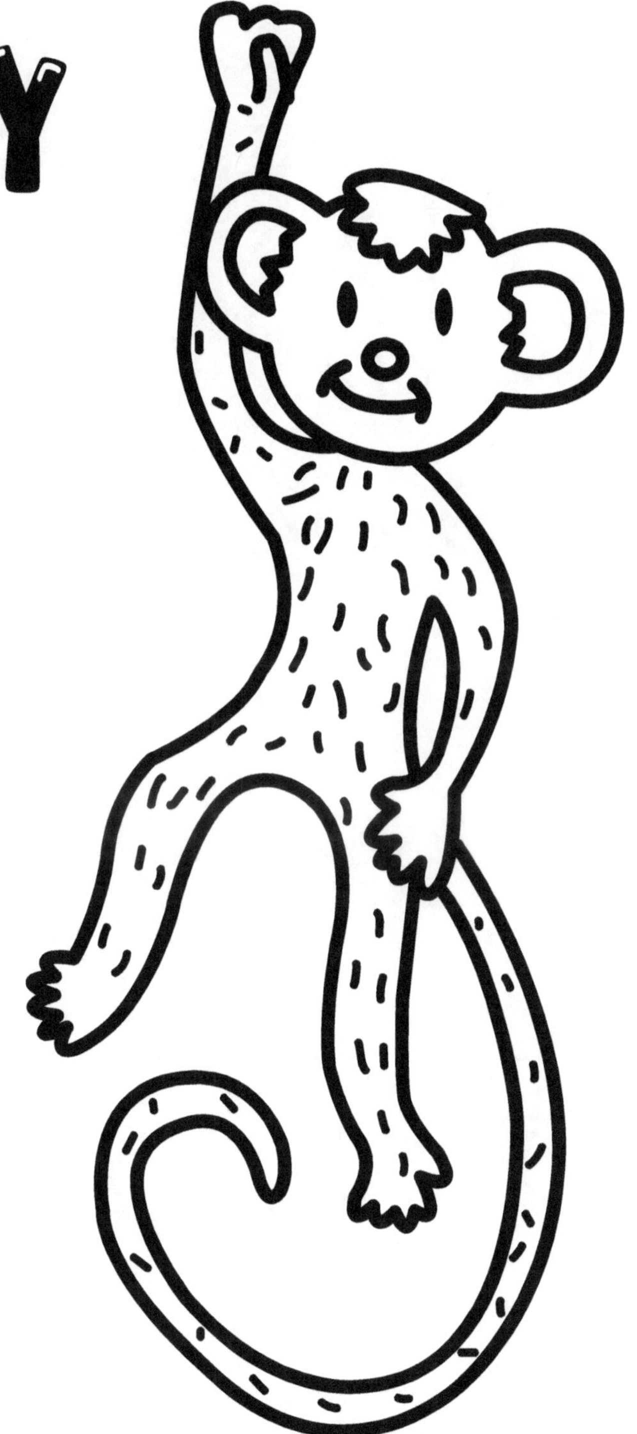

GIRAFFE

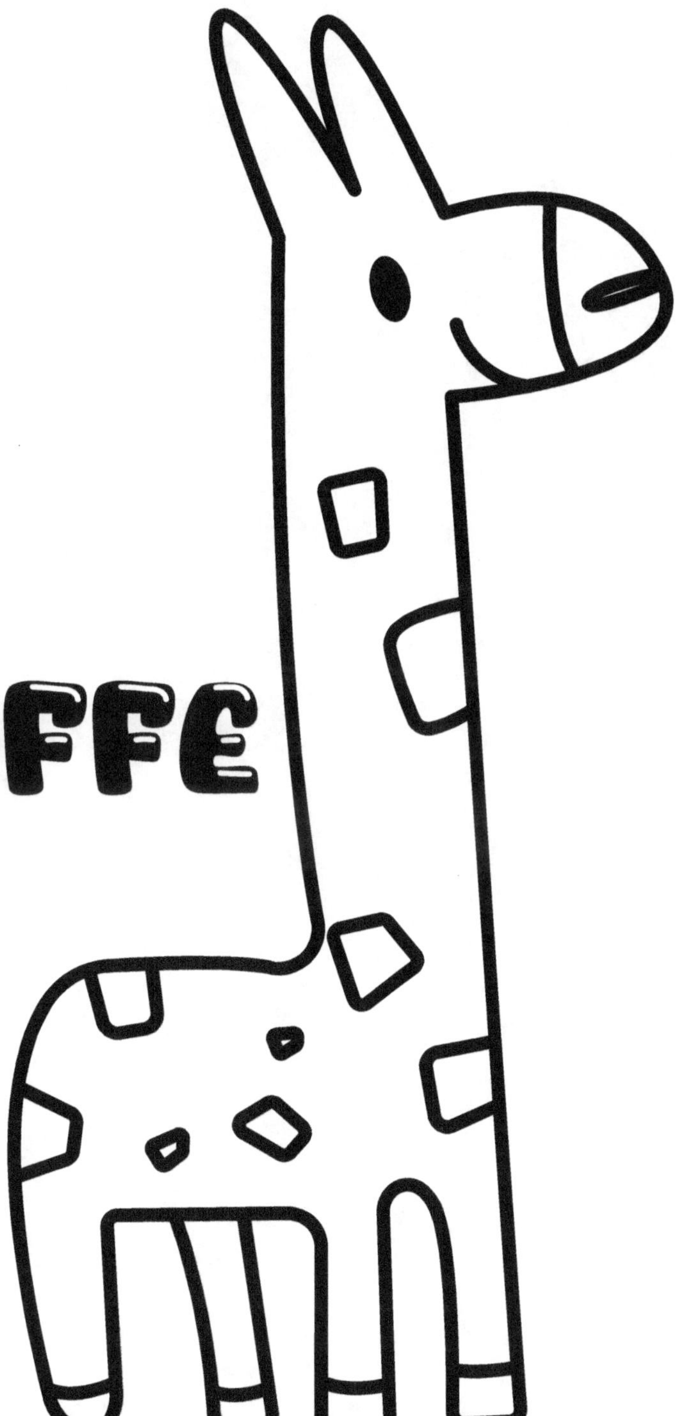

CRAB

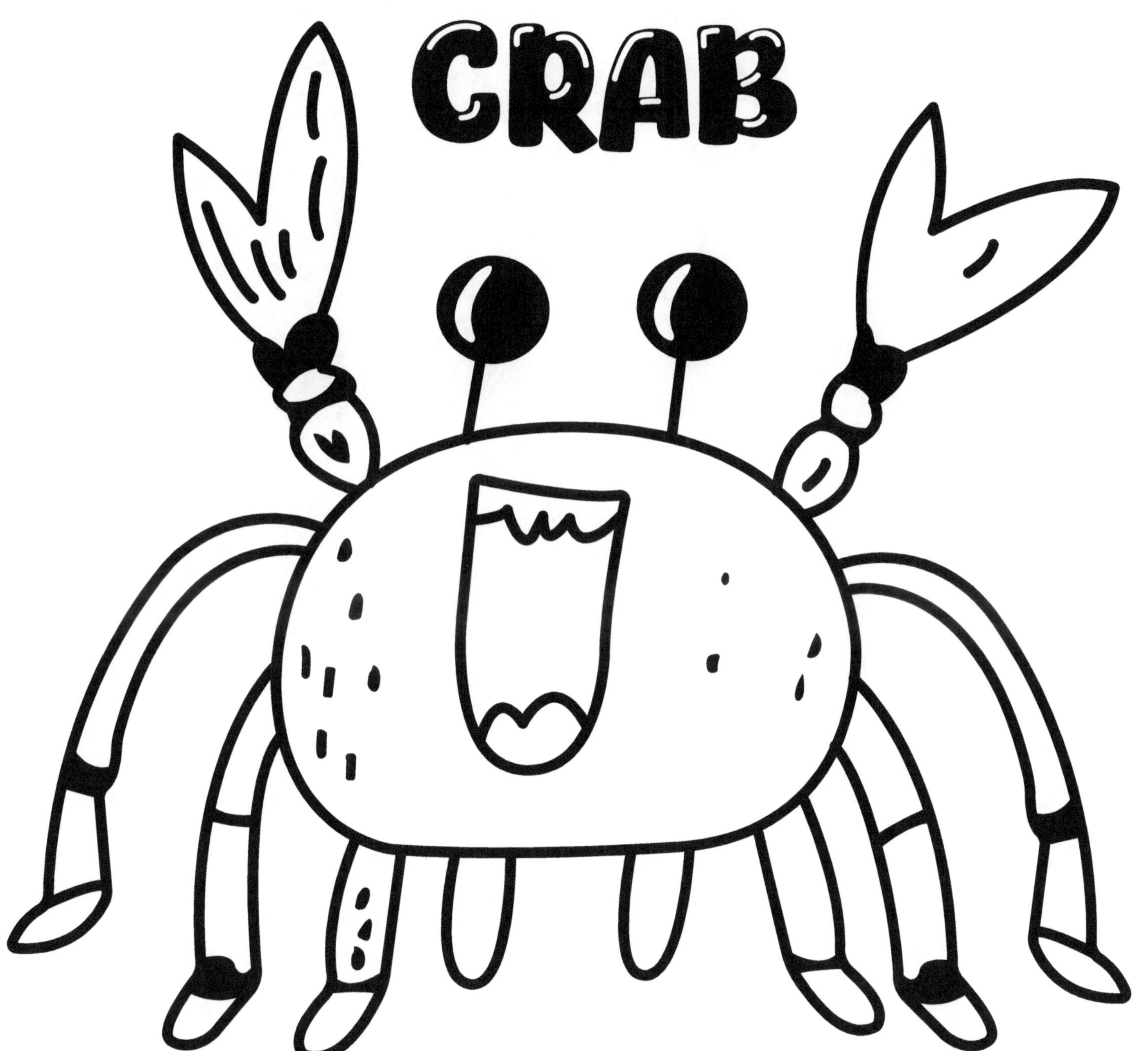

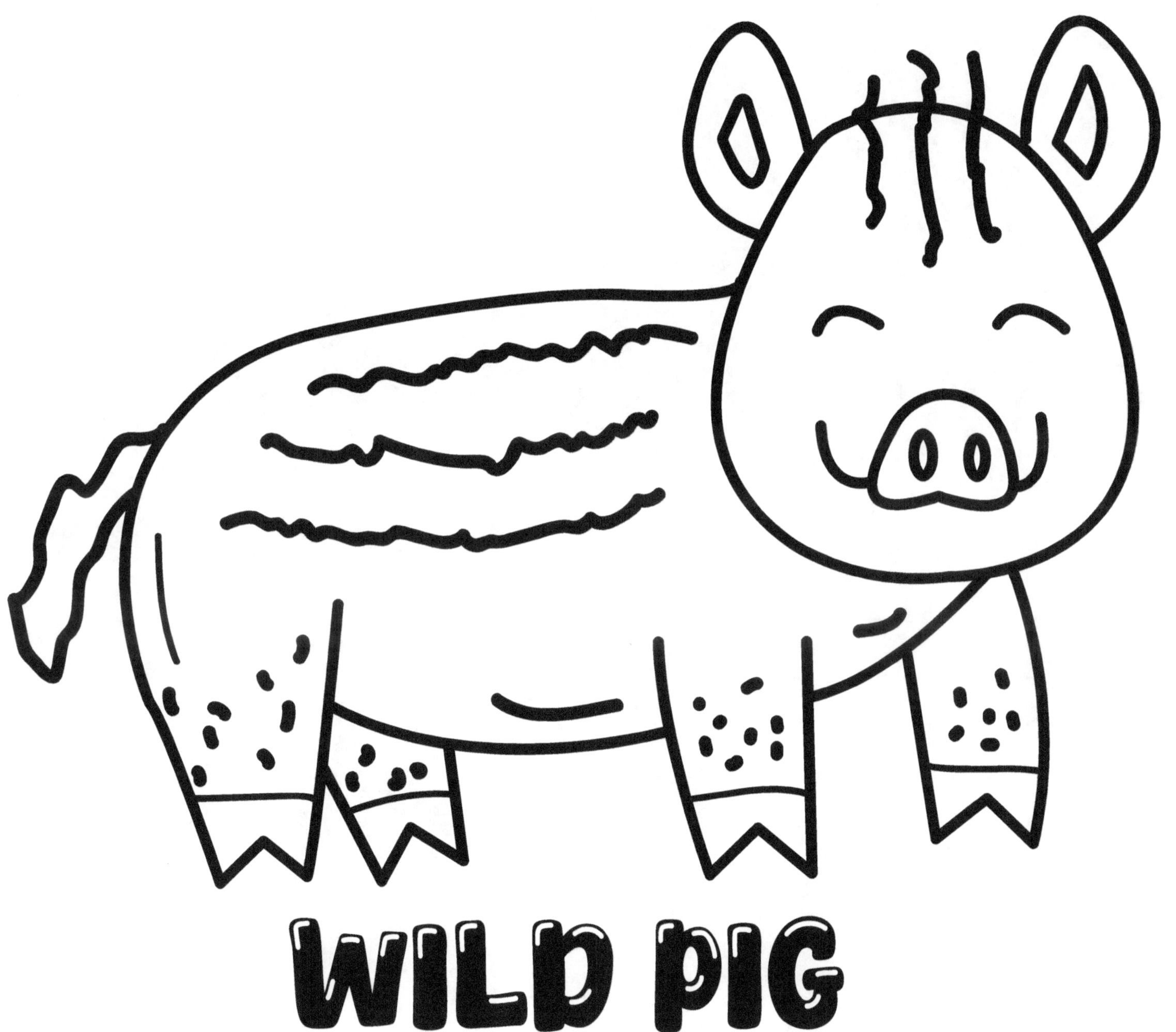

WILD PIG

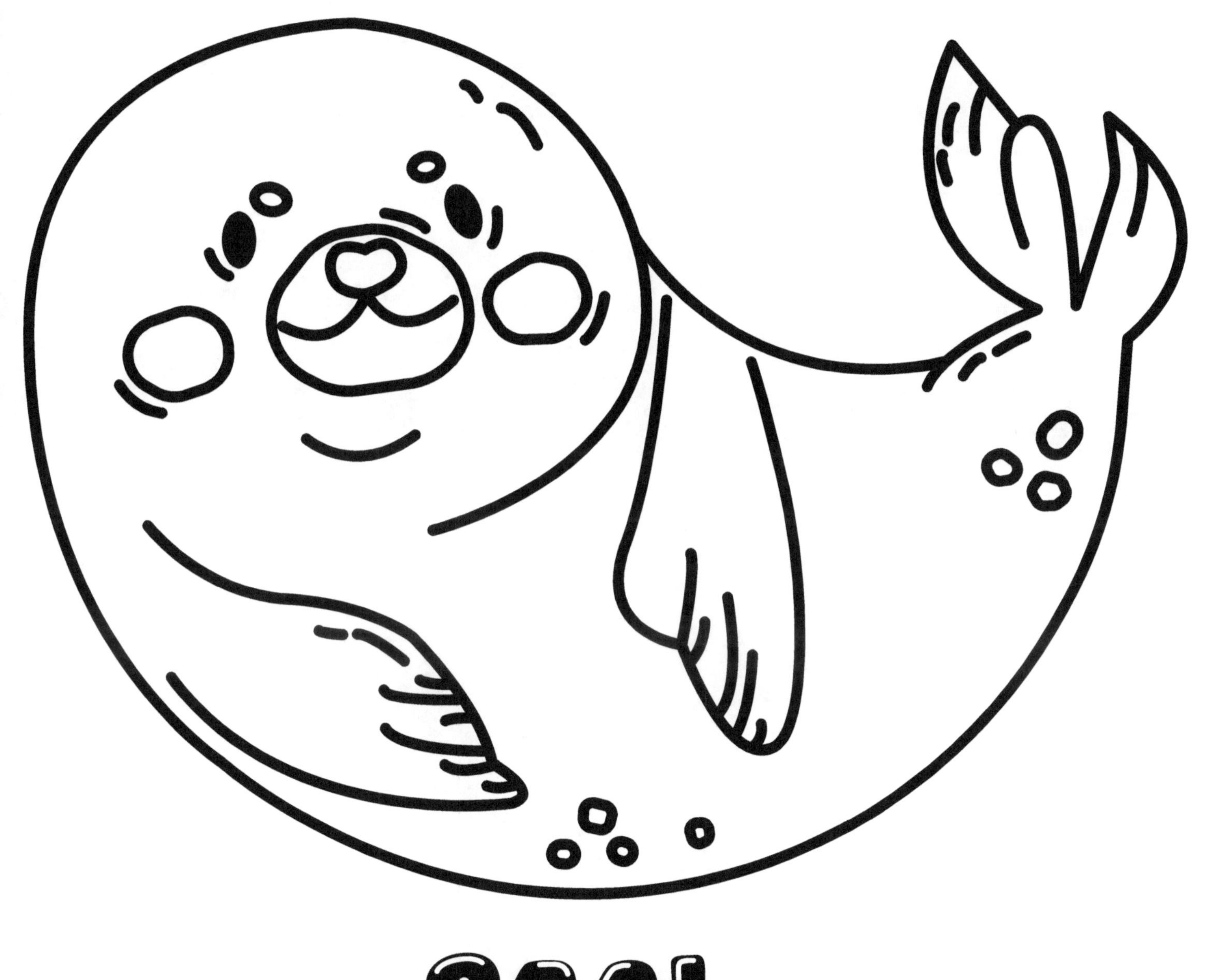

SEAL

LIZARD

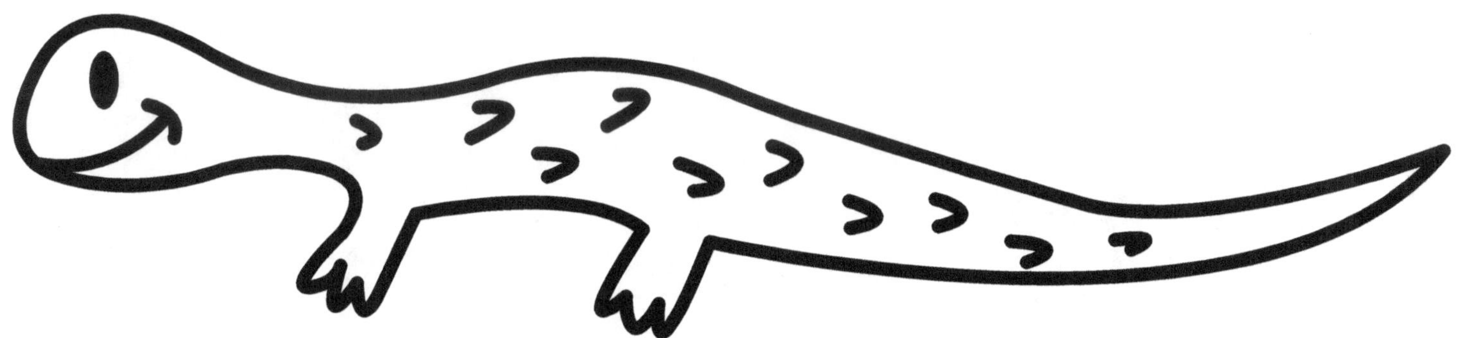

FROG

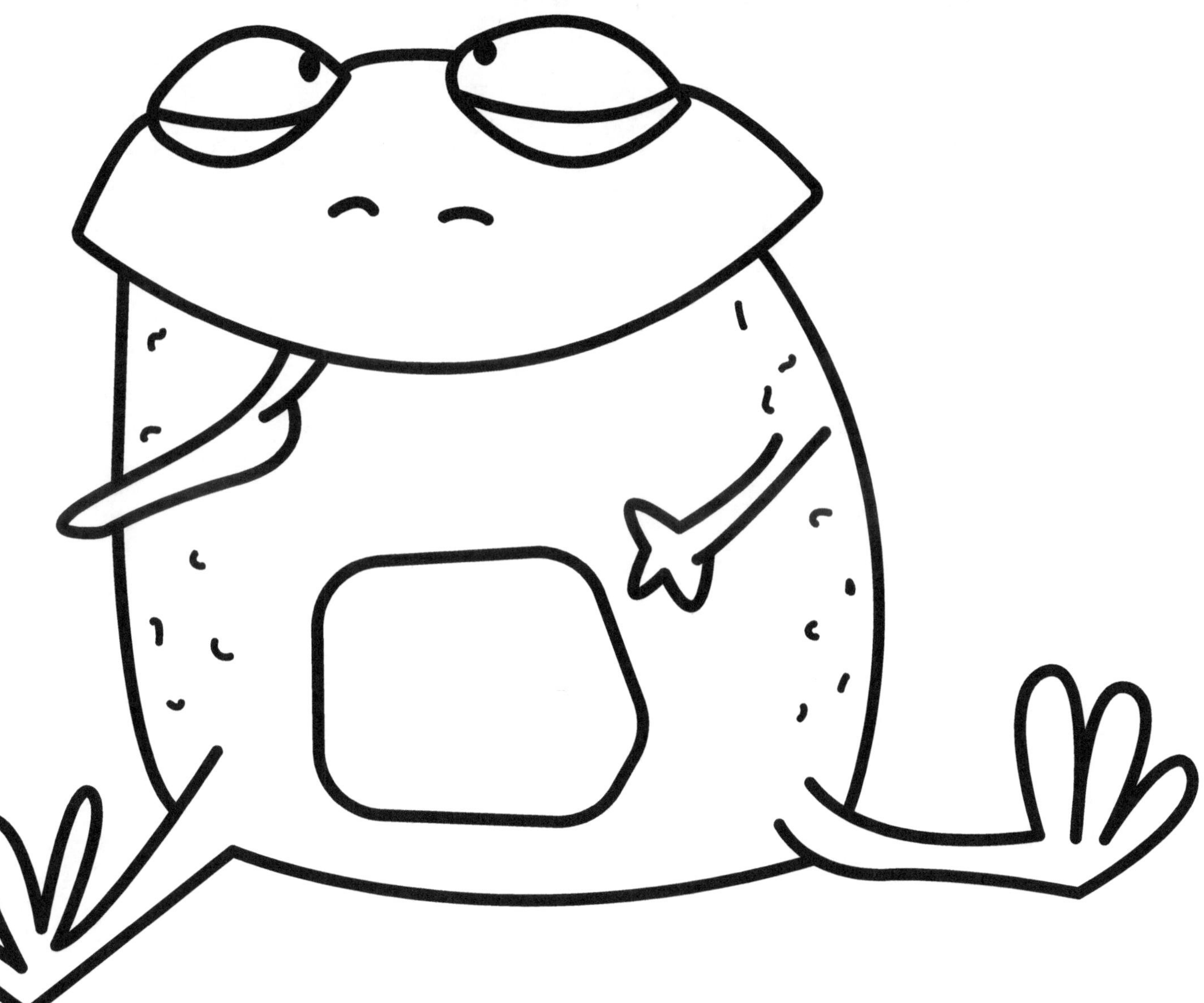

COW

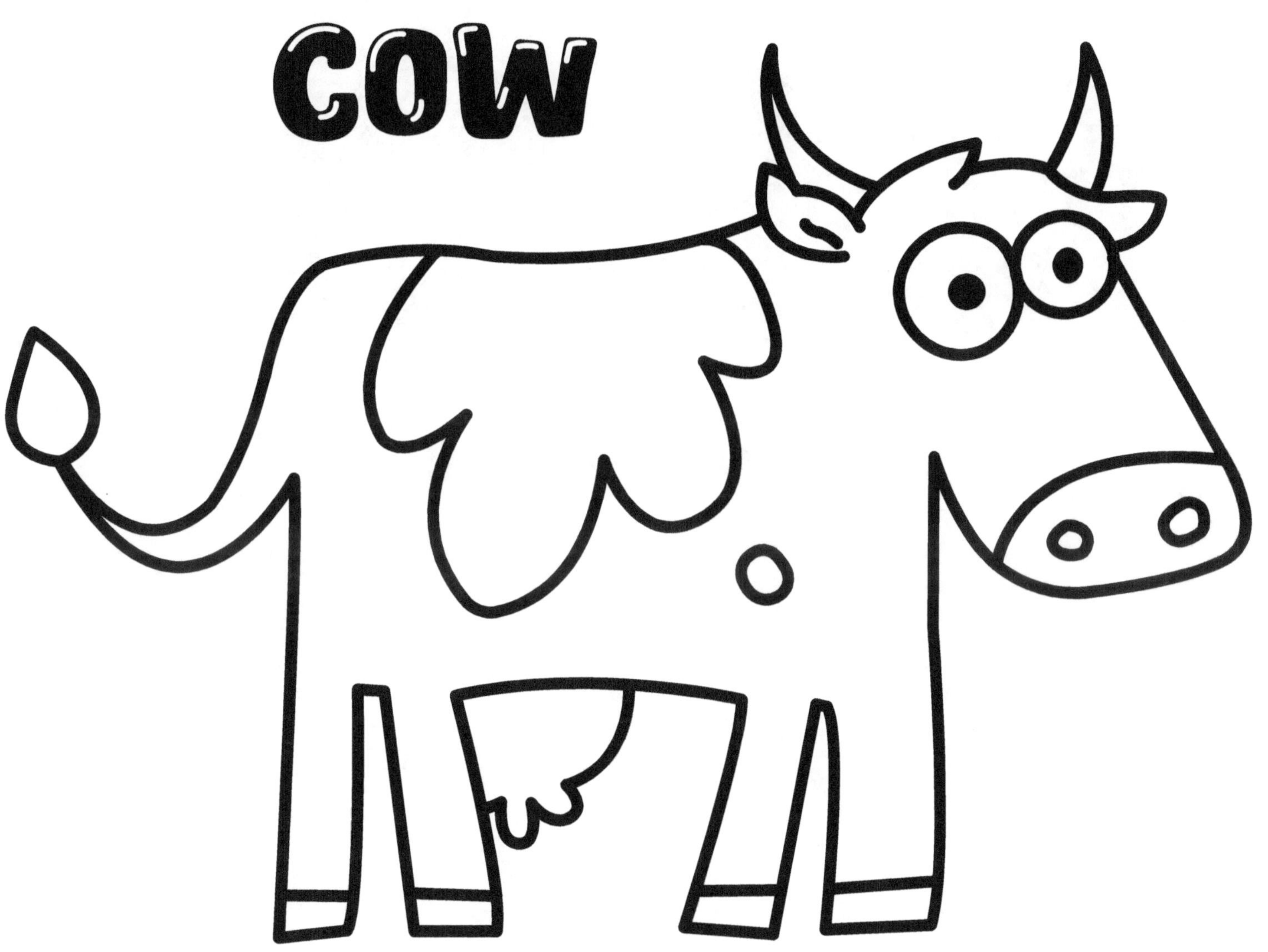

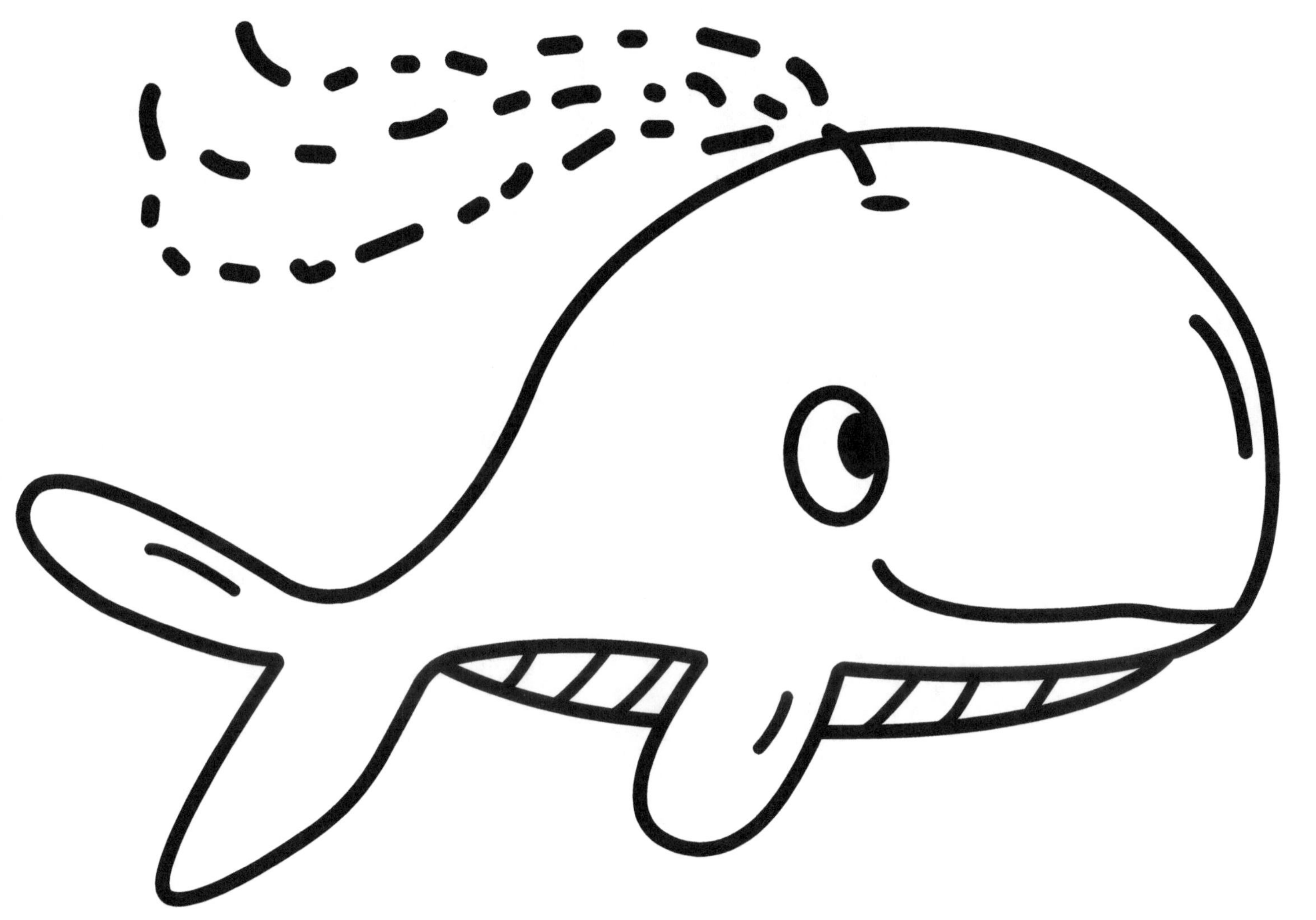

WHALE

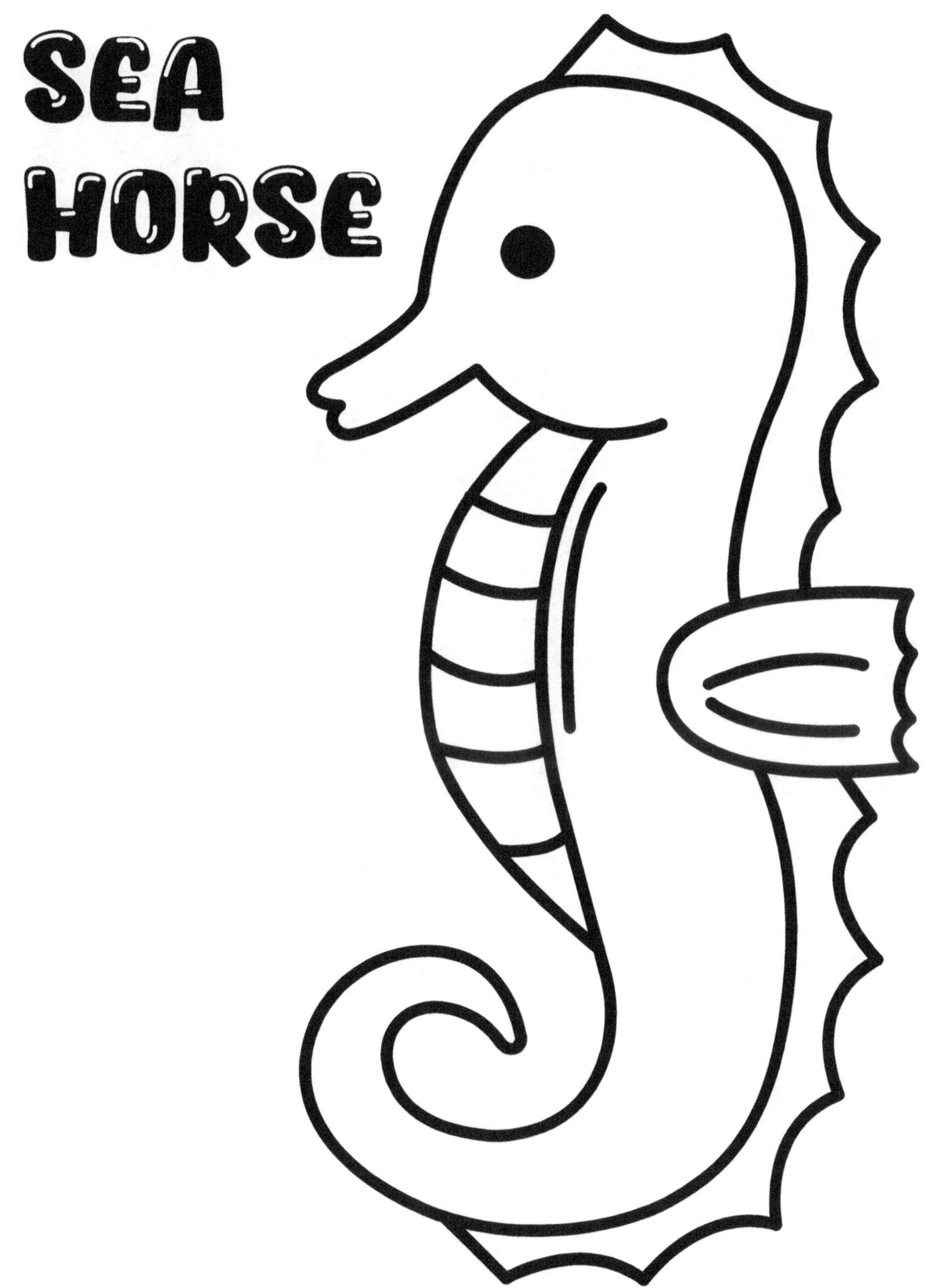

SEA
HORSE

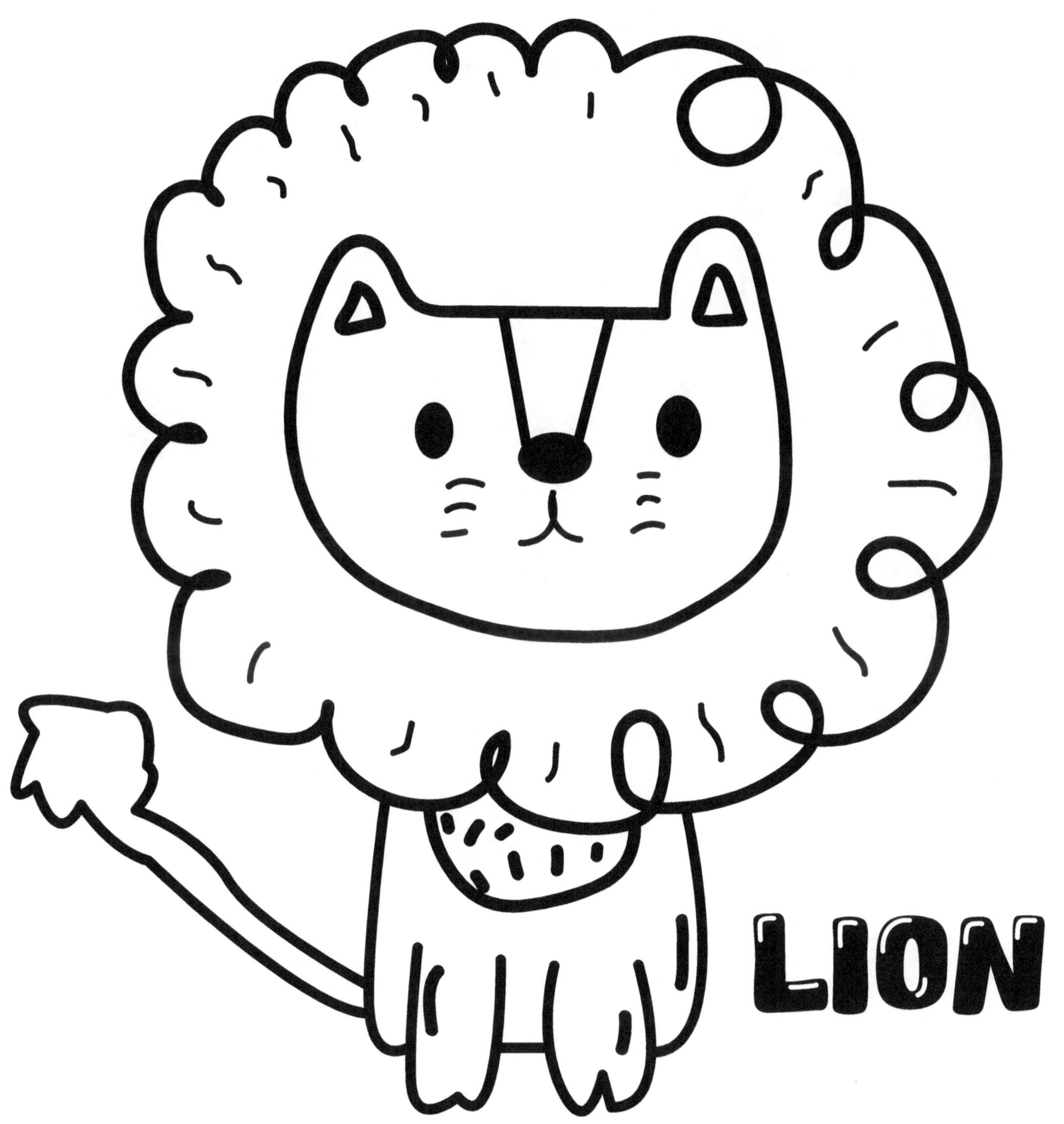

LION

FOX

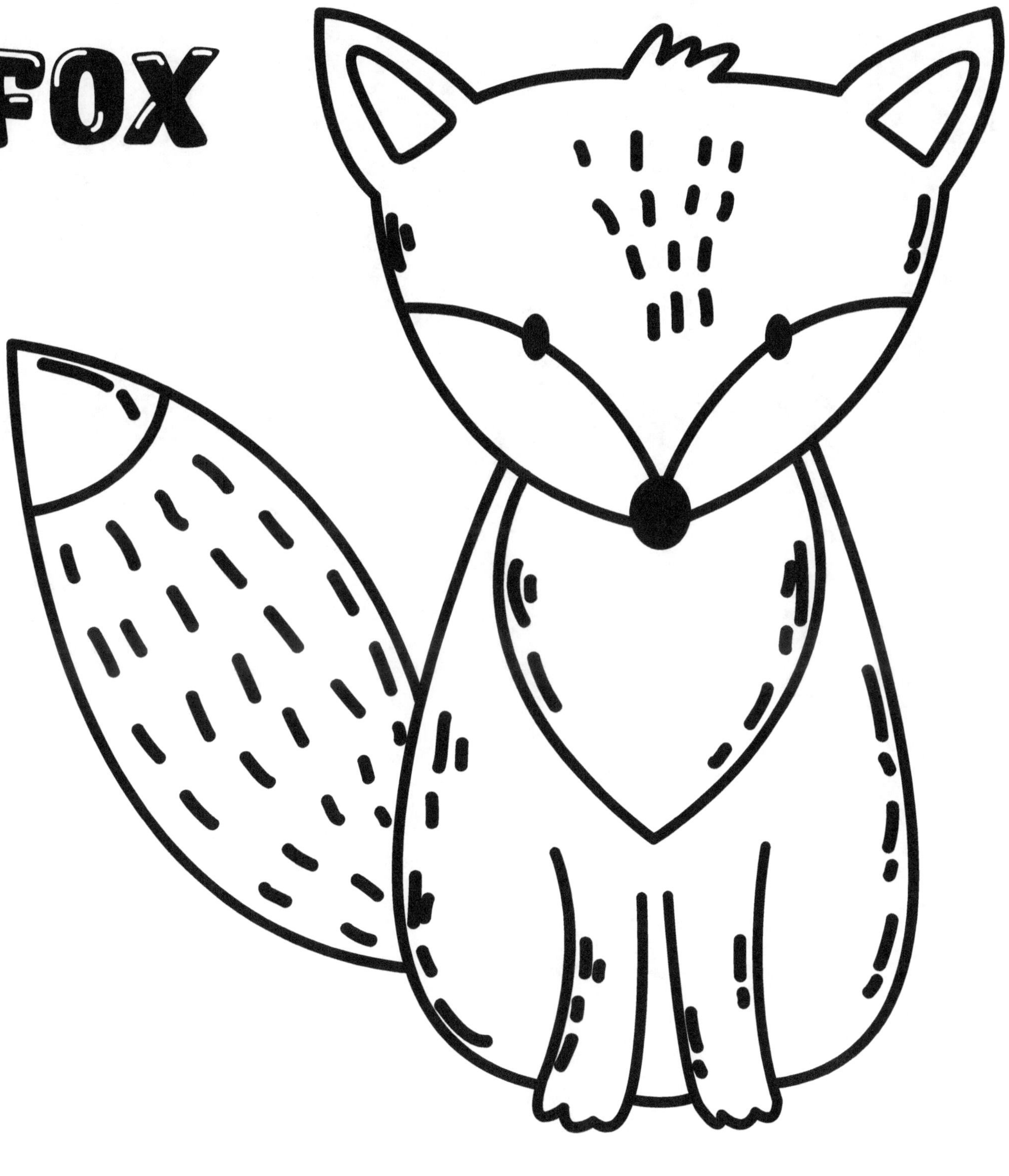

FOX

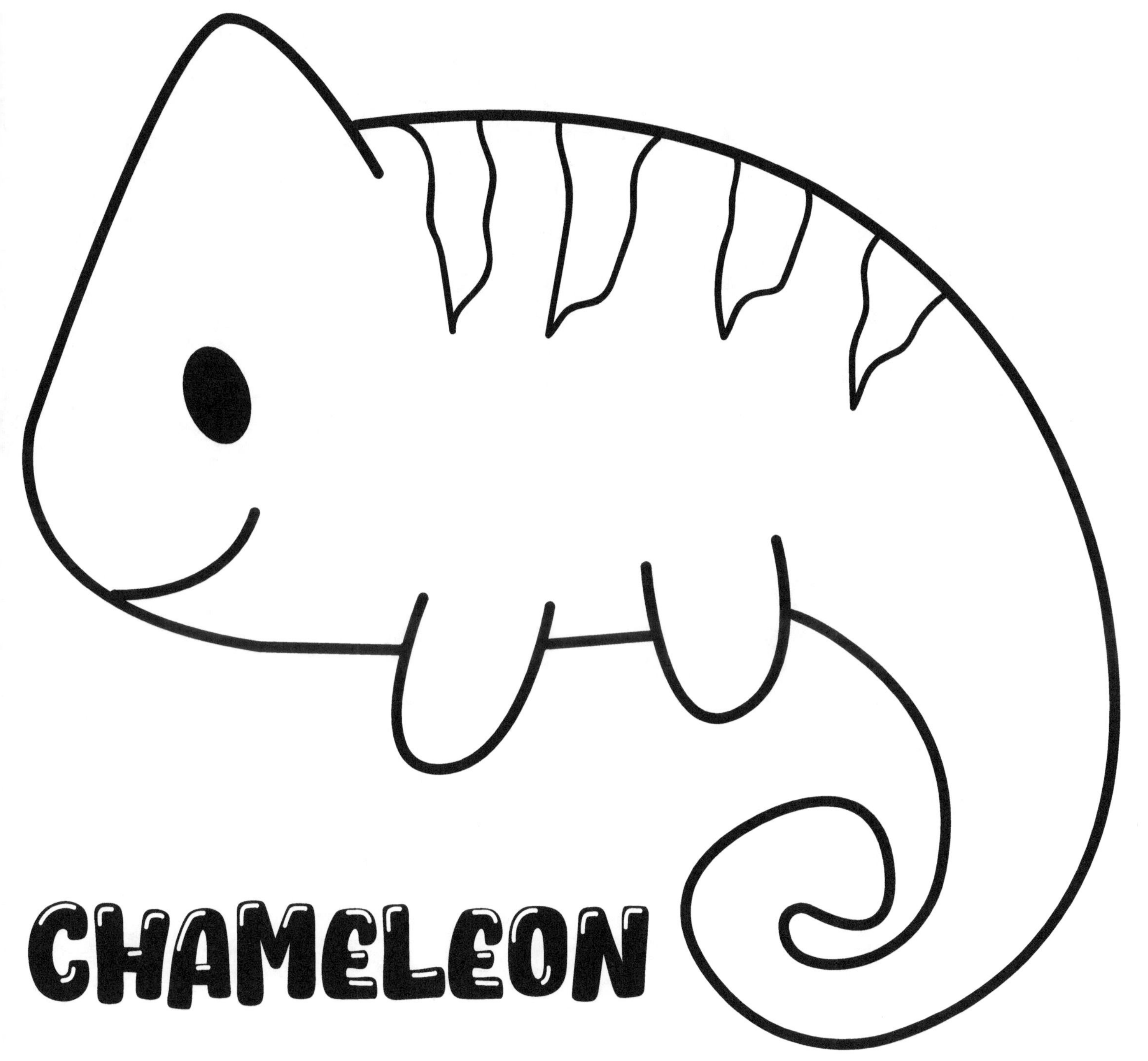
CHAMELEON

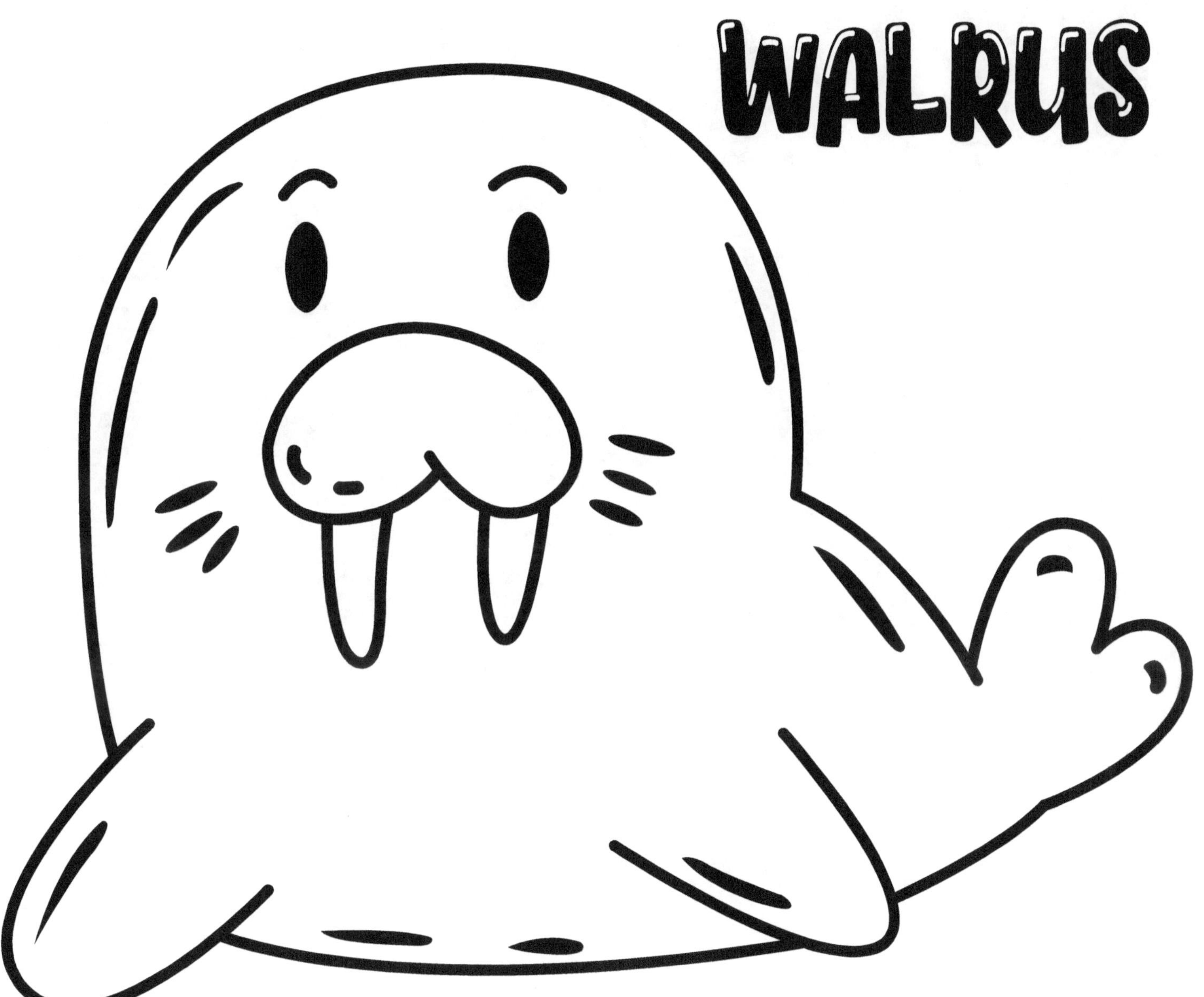

WALRUS

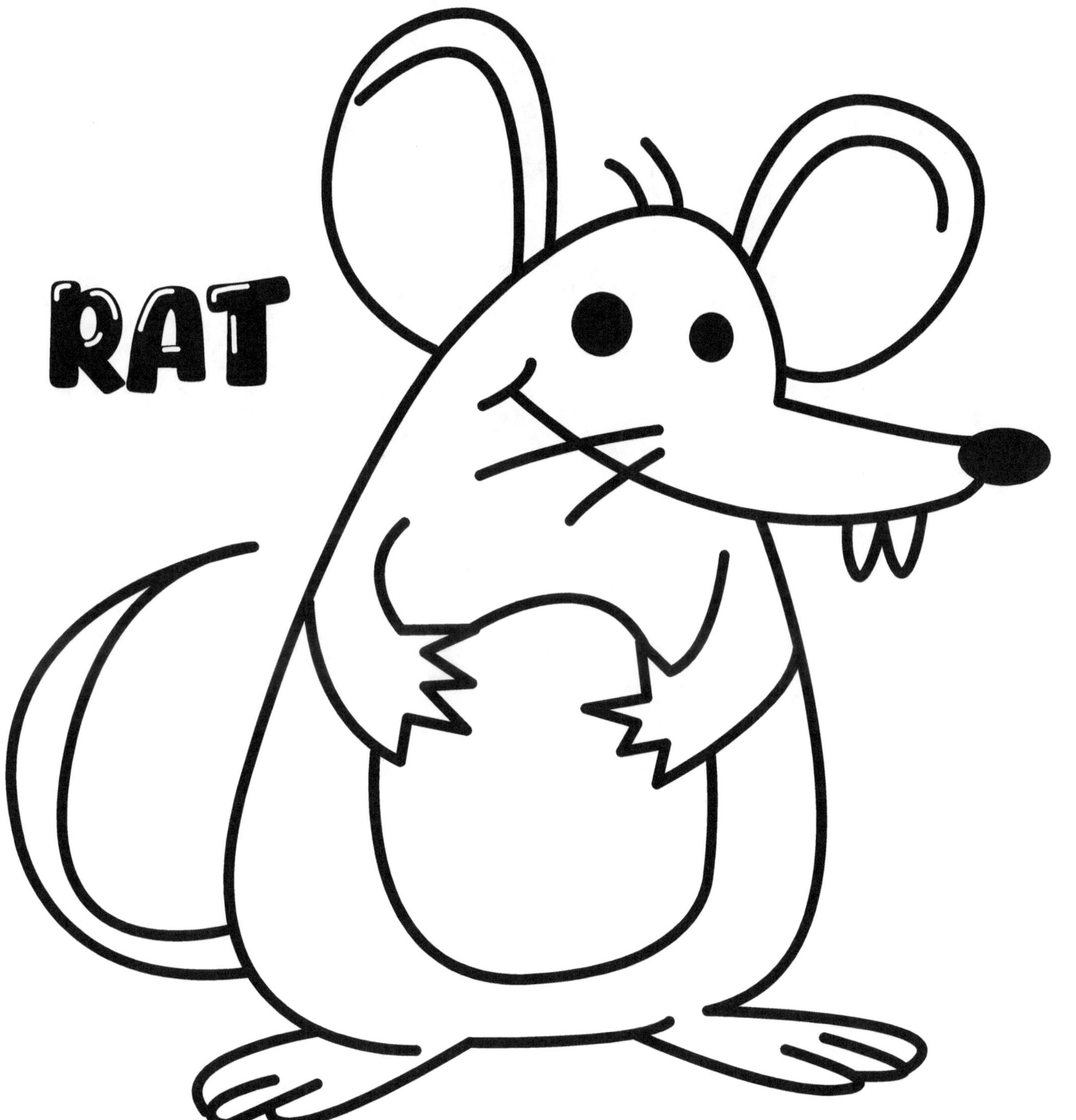
RAT

LANTERN FISH

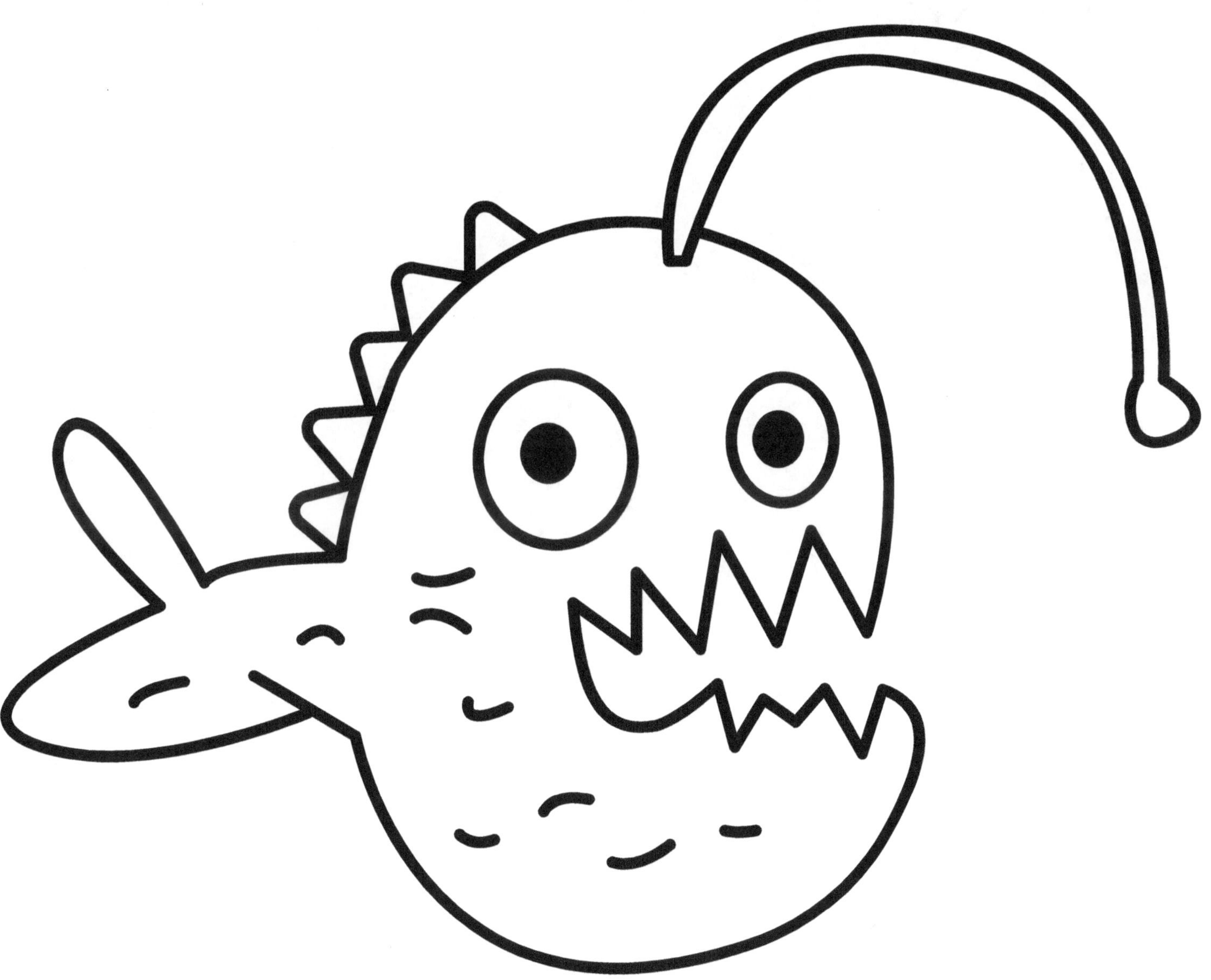

FISH

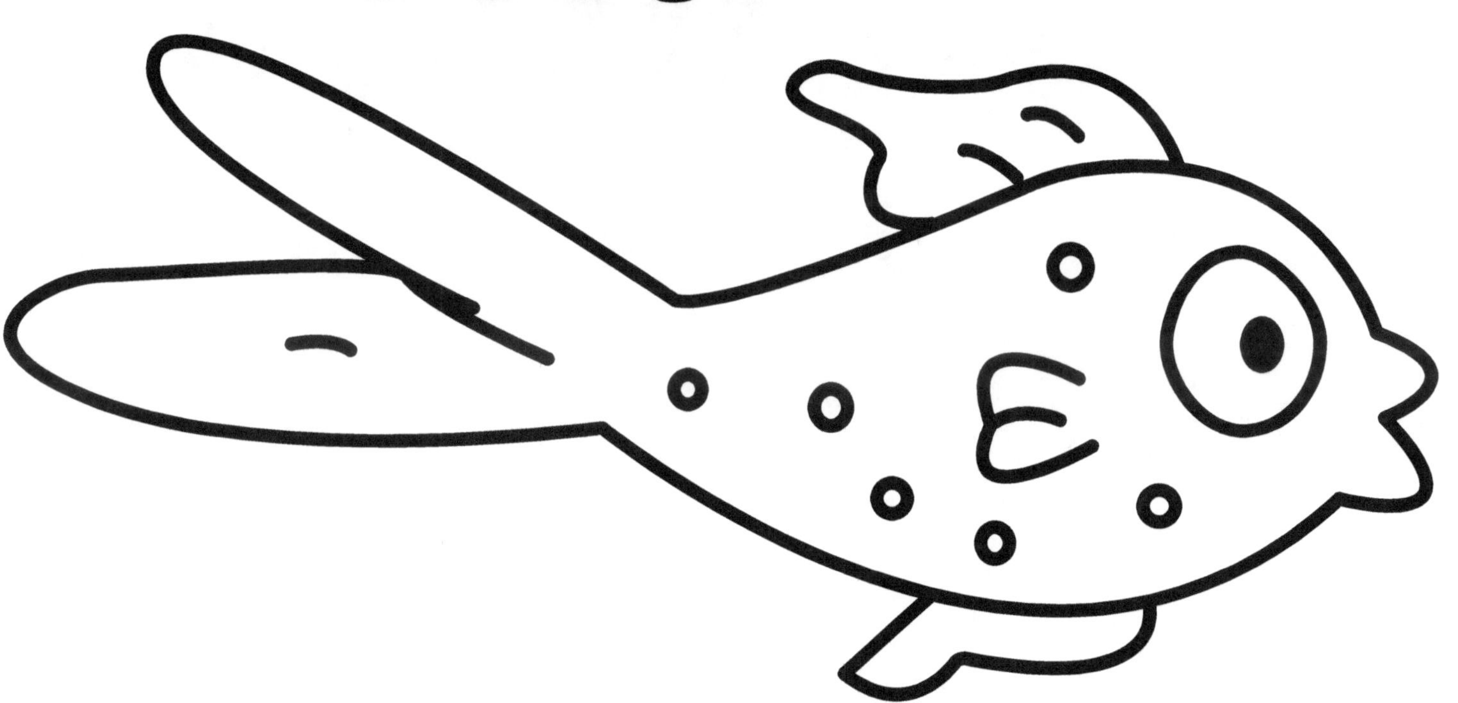

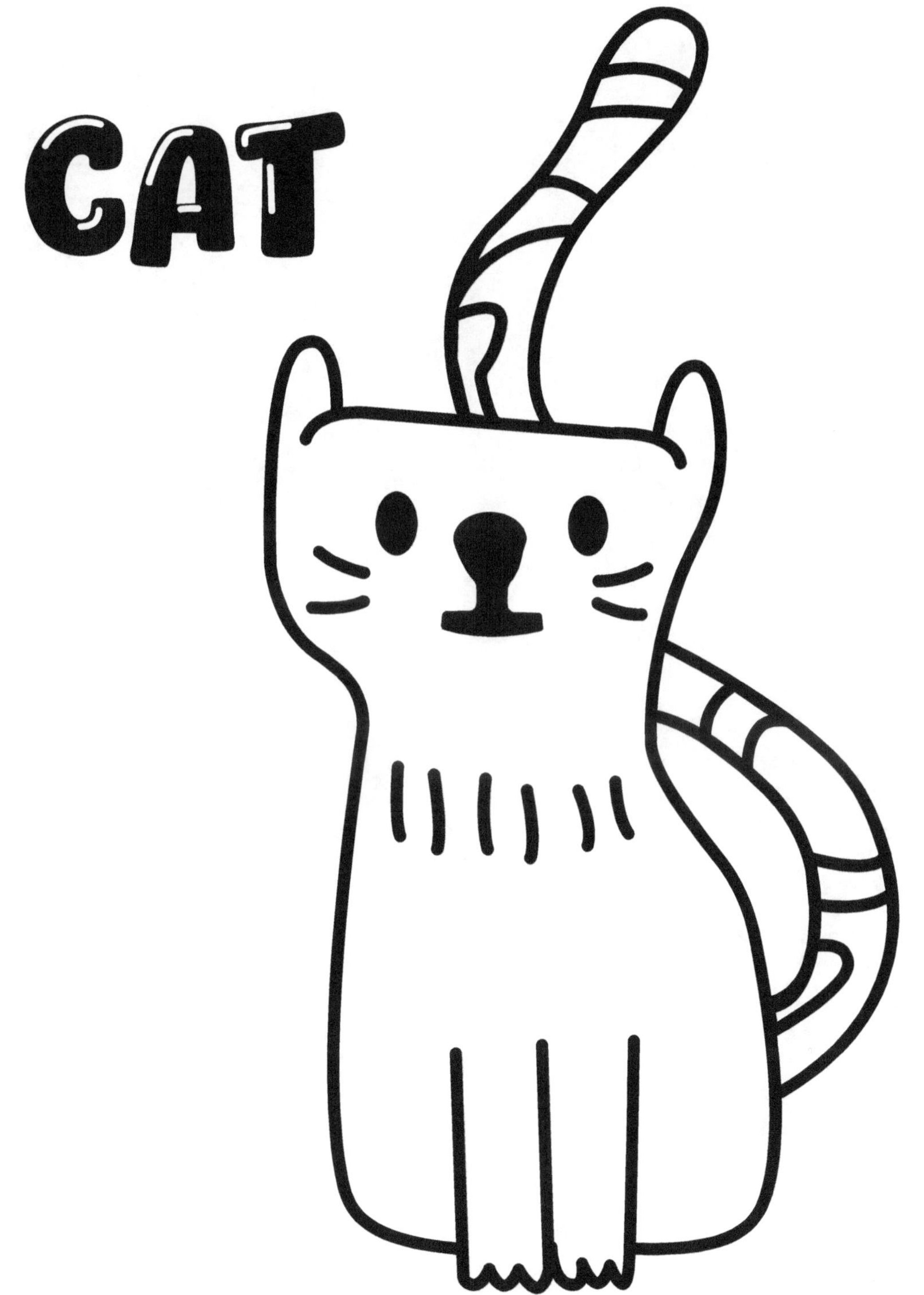
CAT

TURTLE

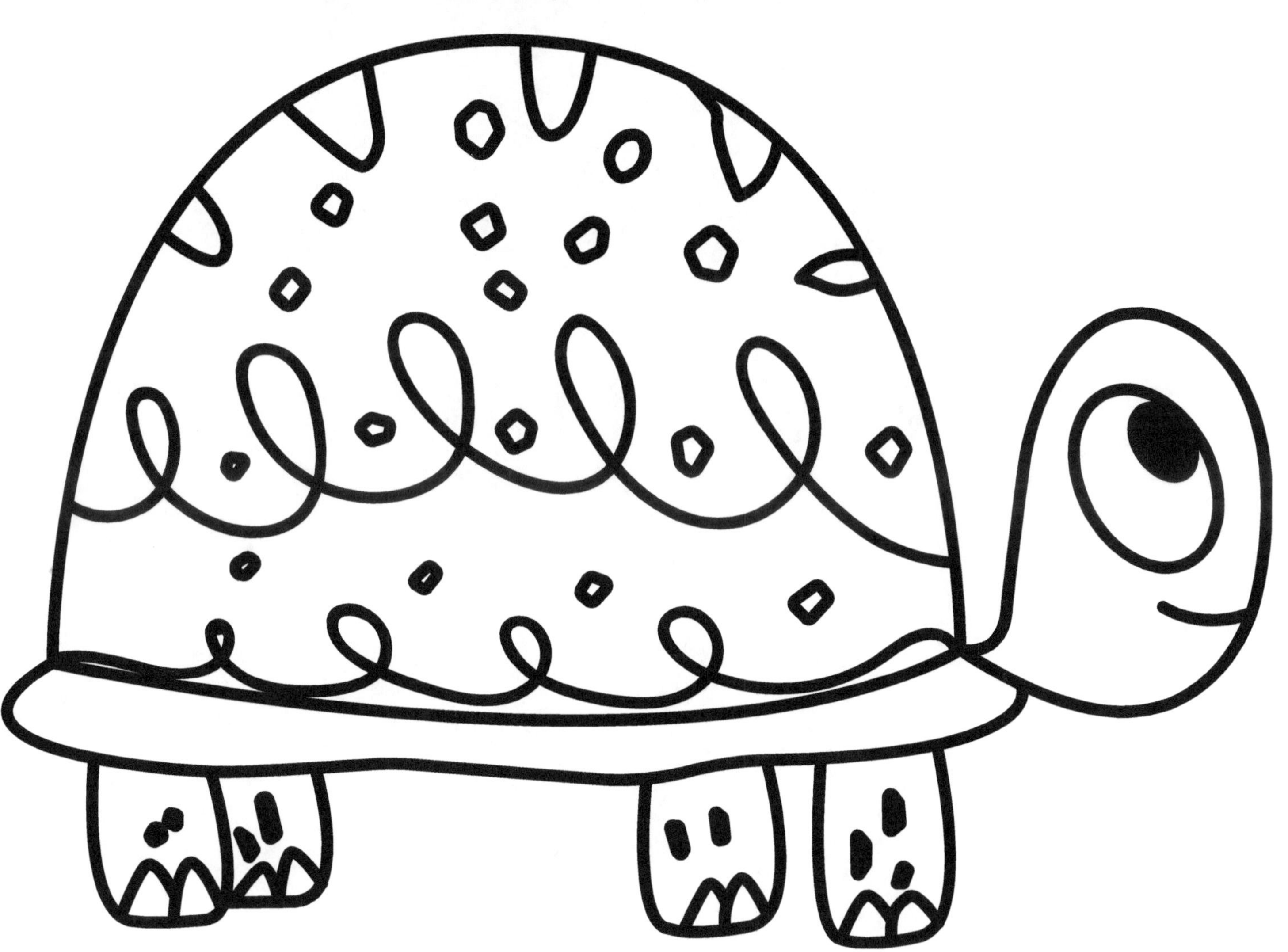

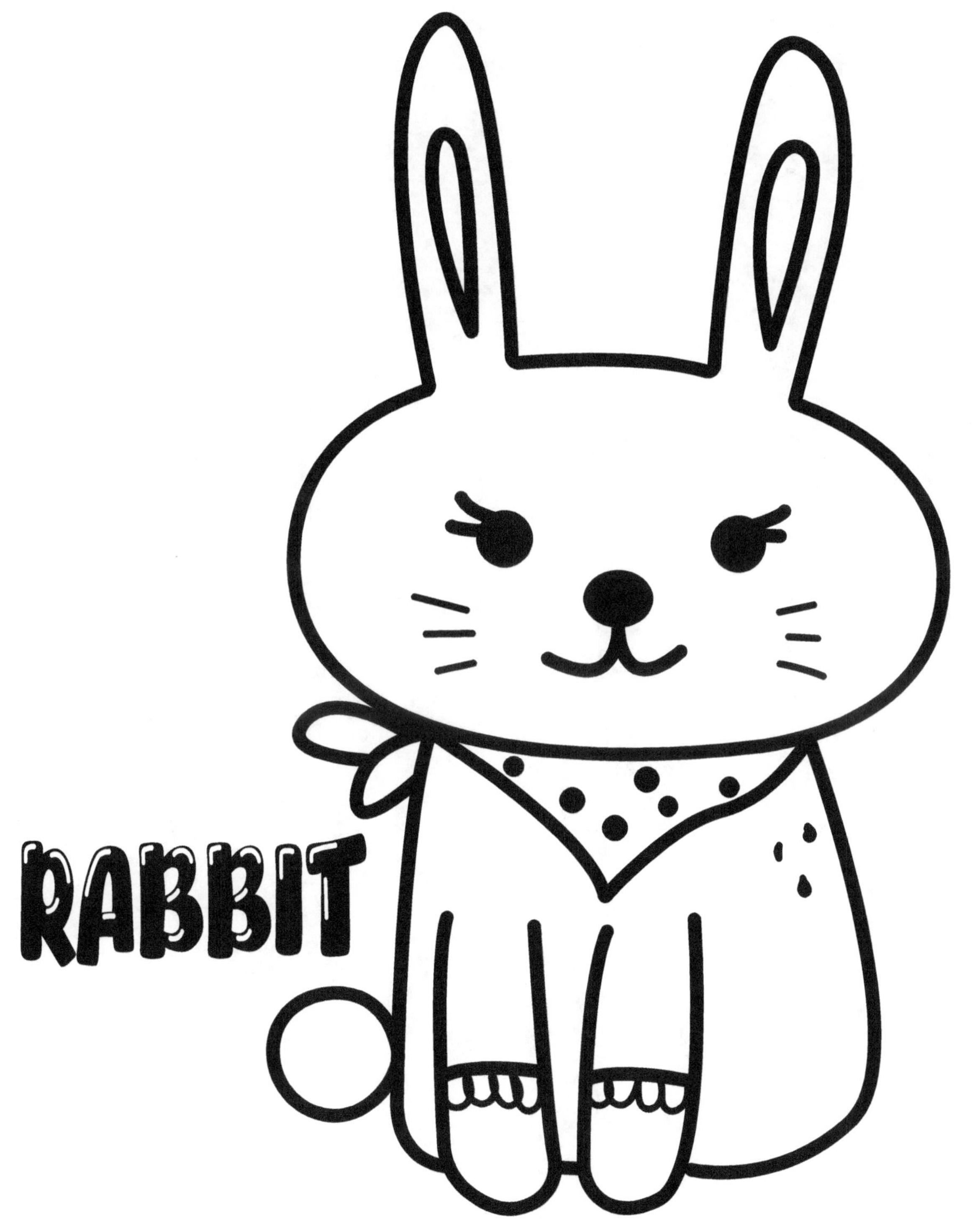
RABBIT

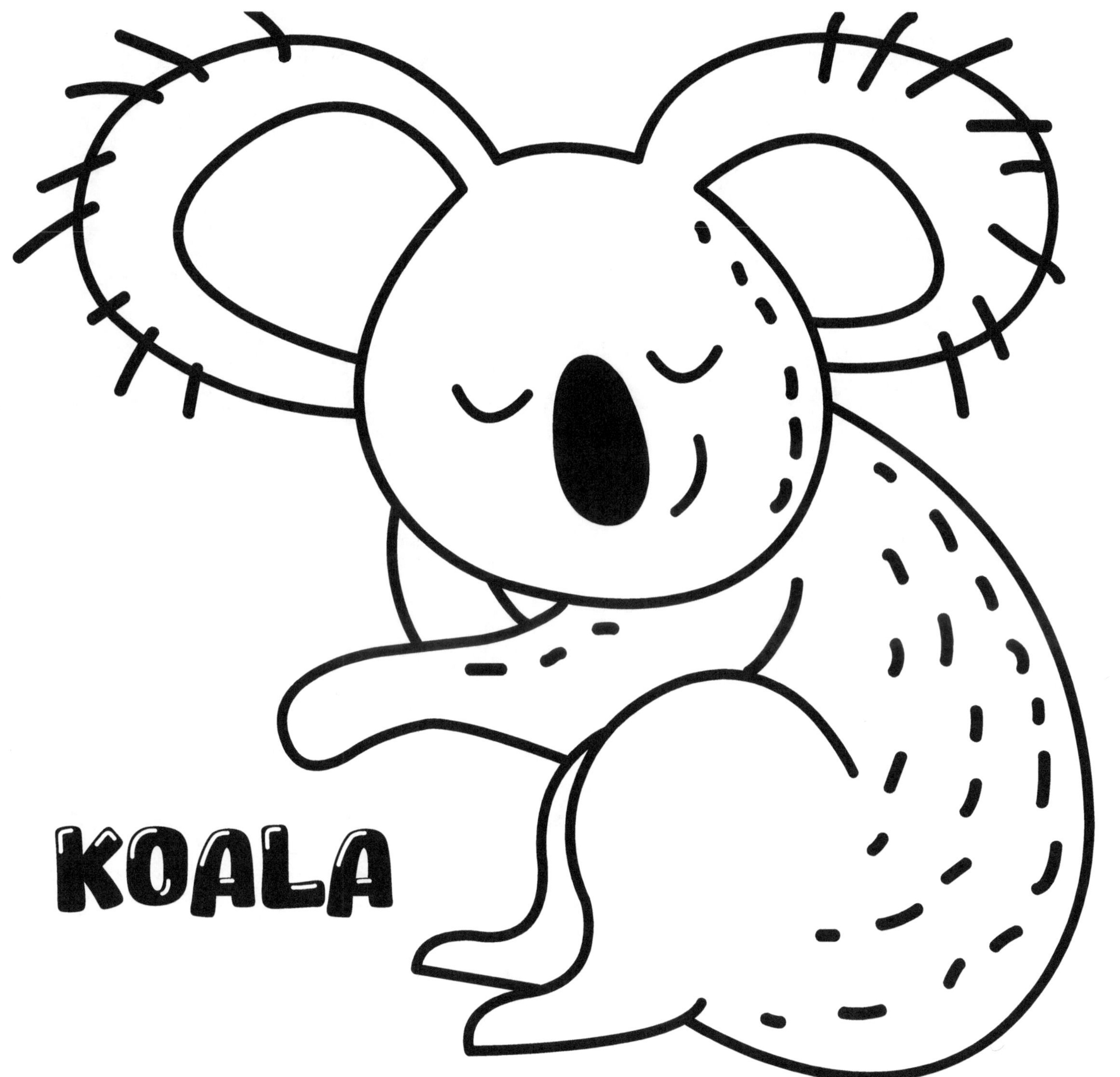
KOALA

ELEPHANT

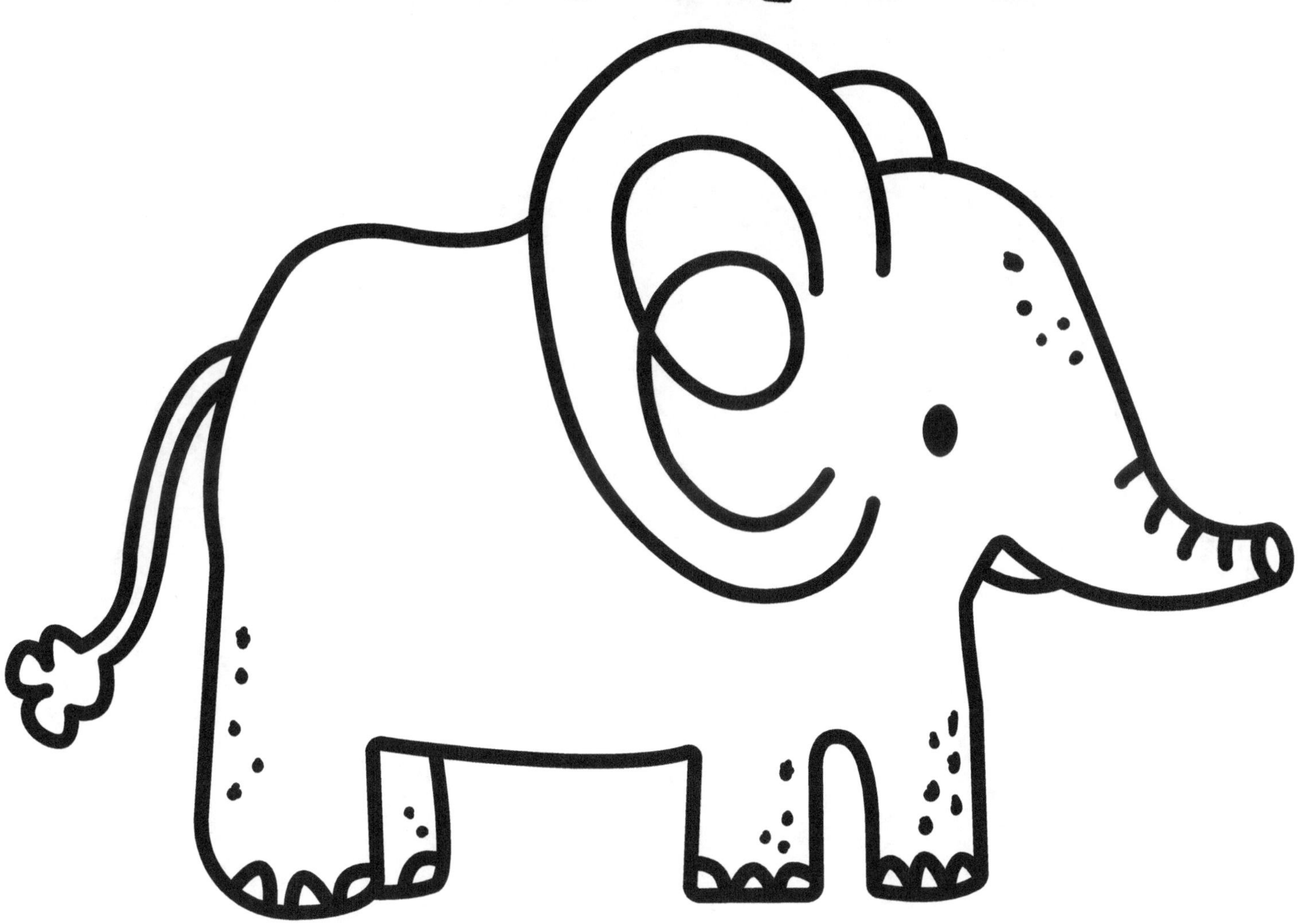

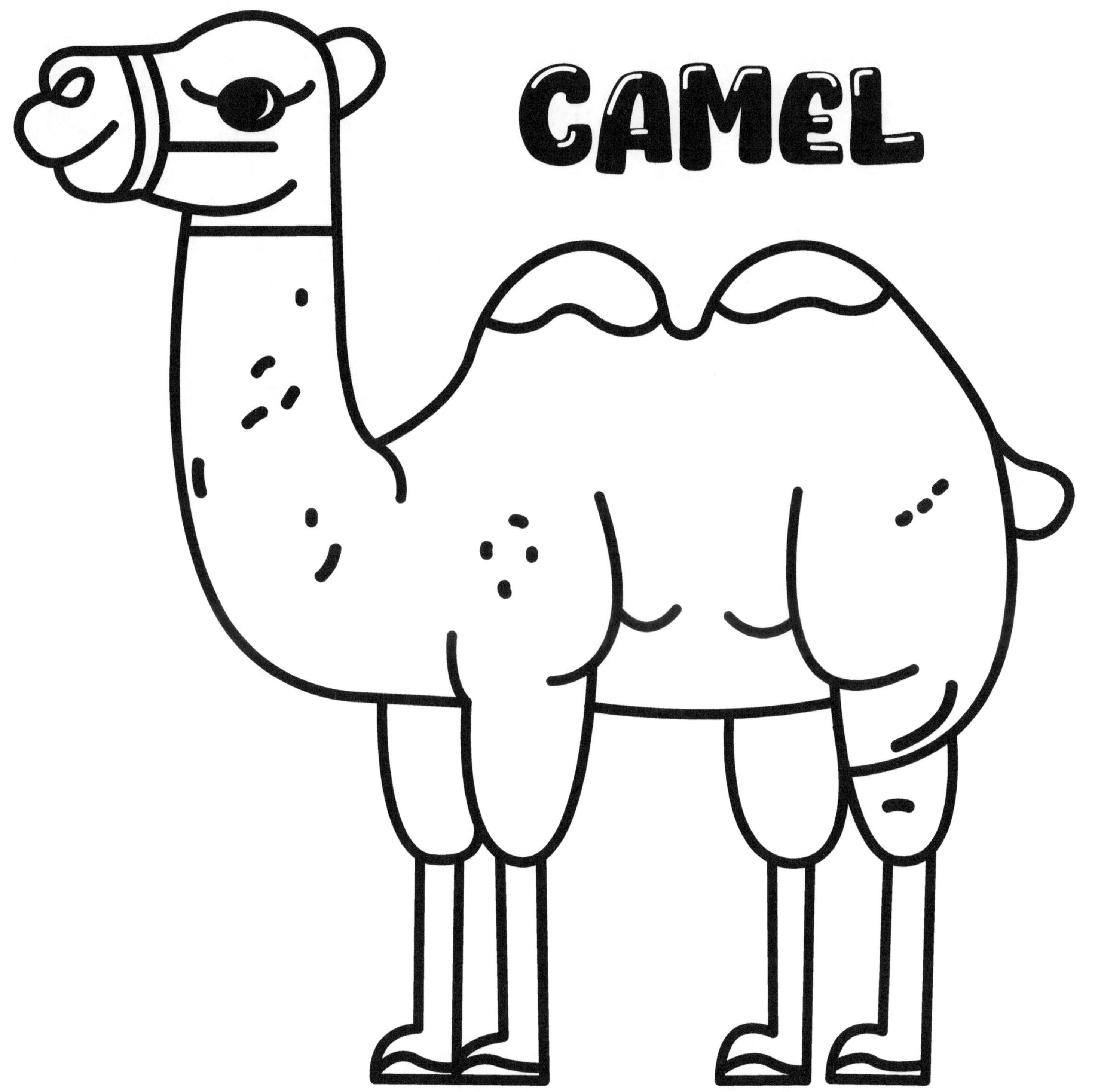

CAMEL

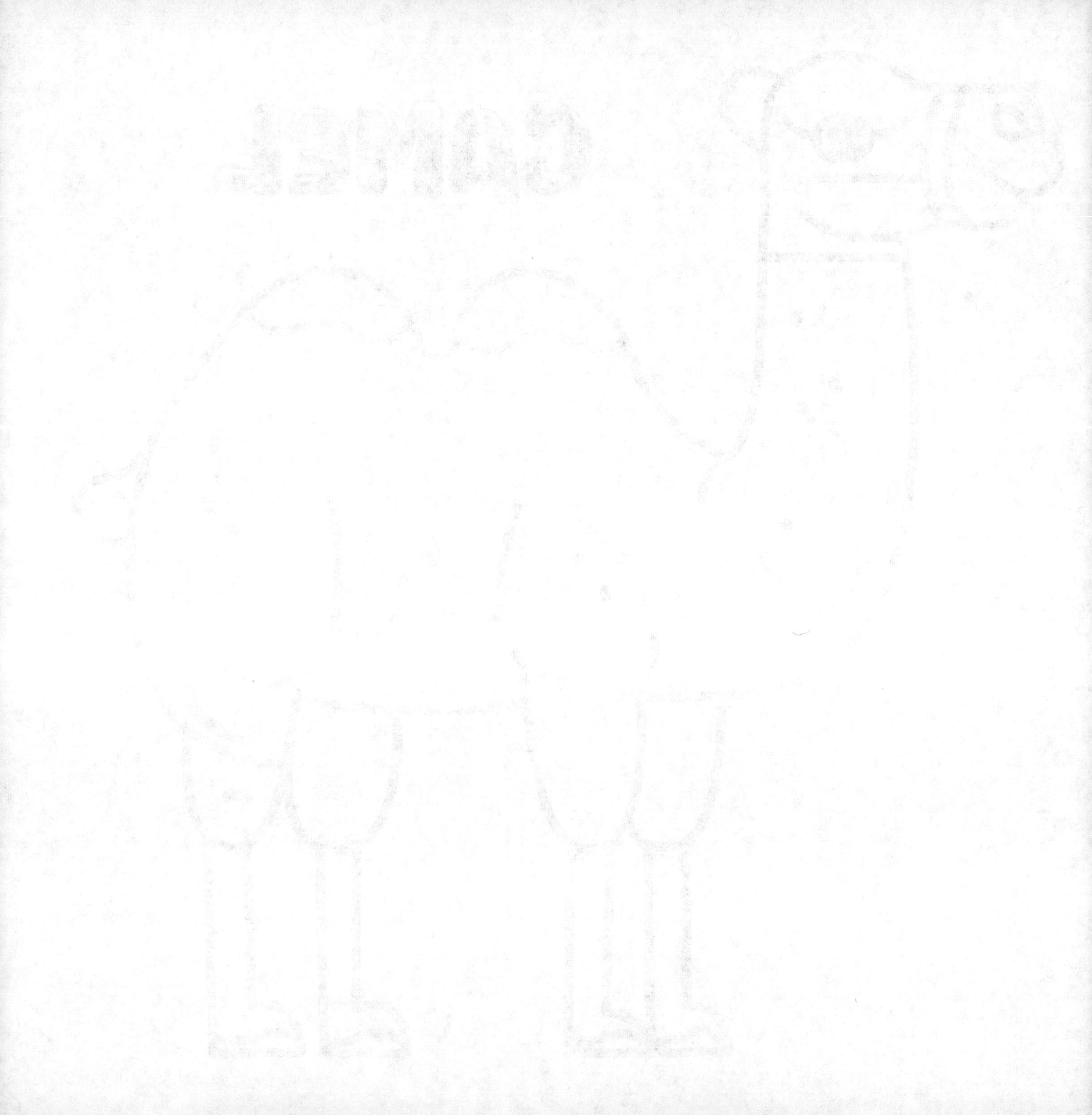

TIGER

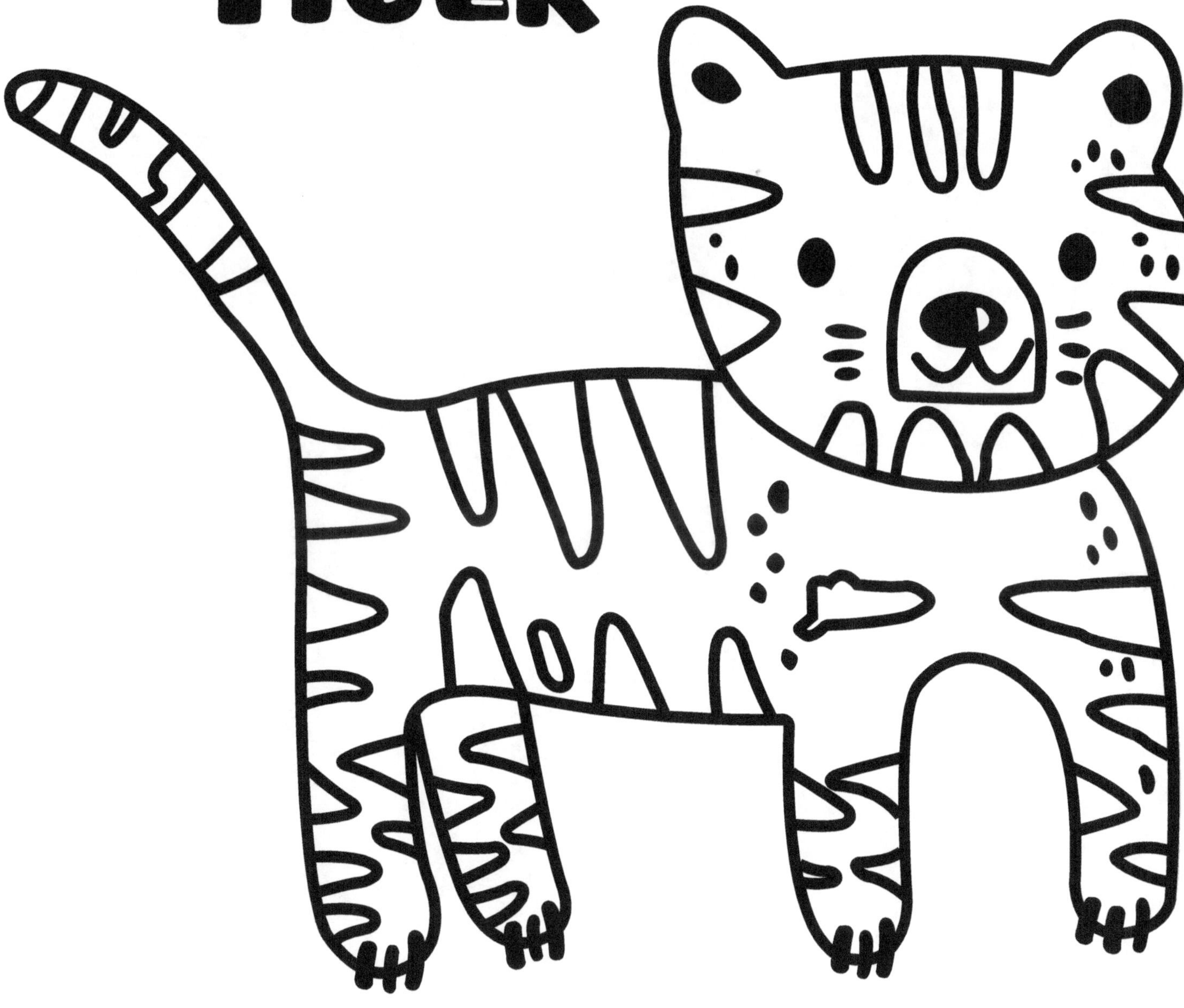

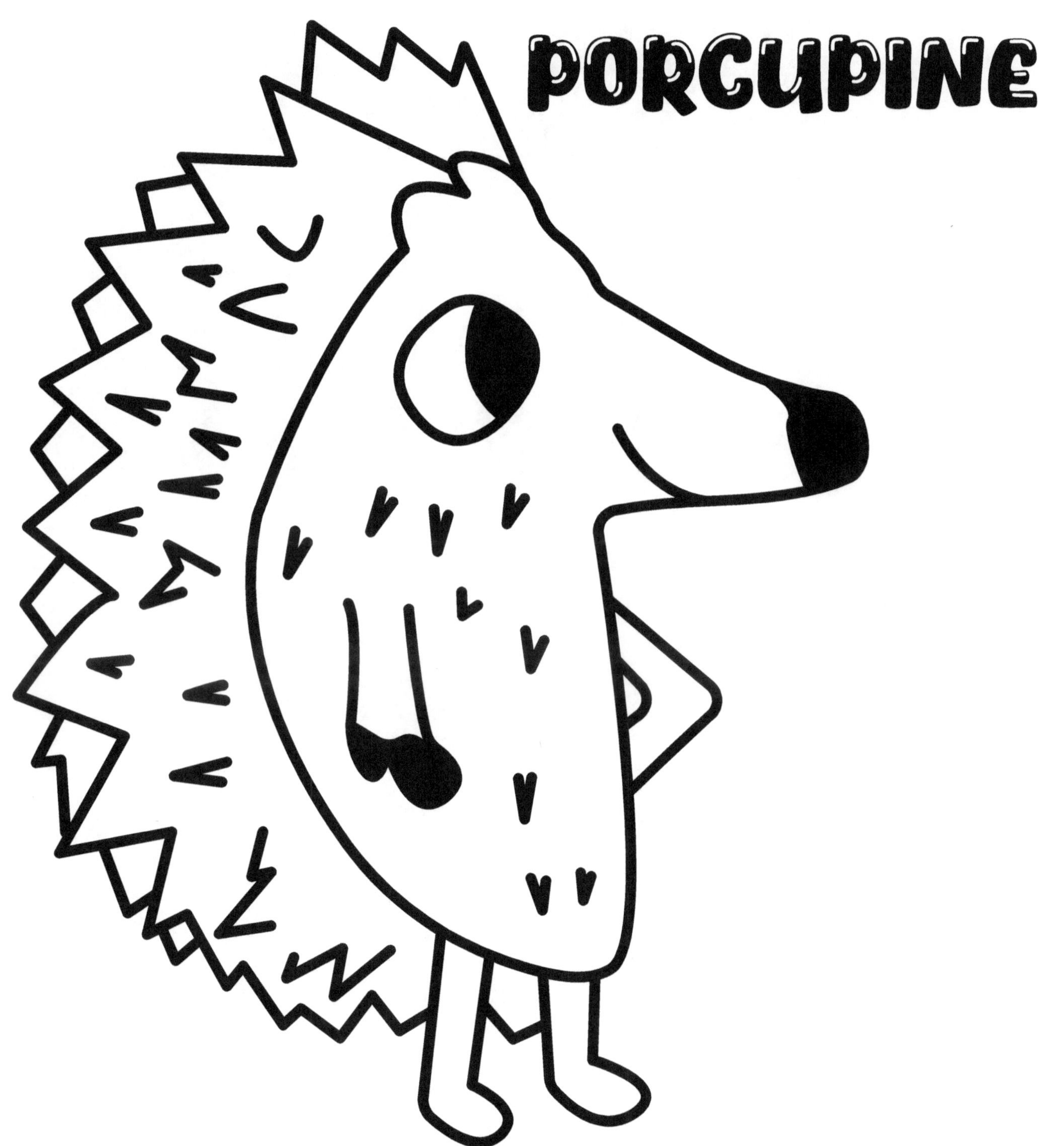

PORCUPINE

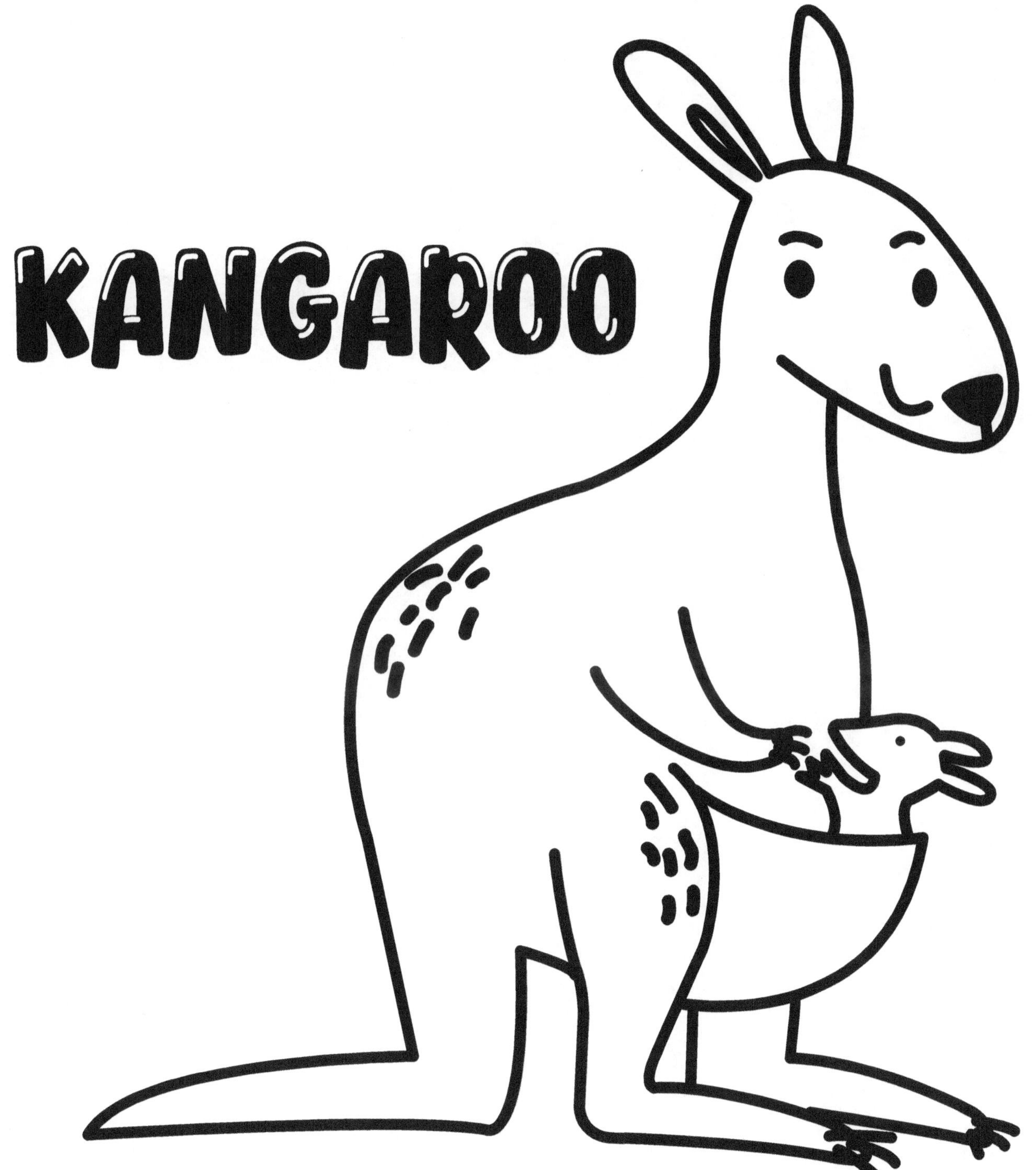

KANGAROO

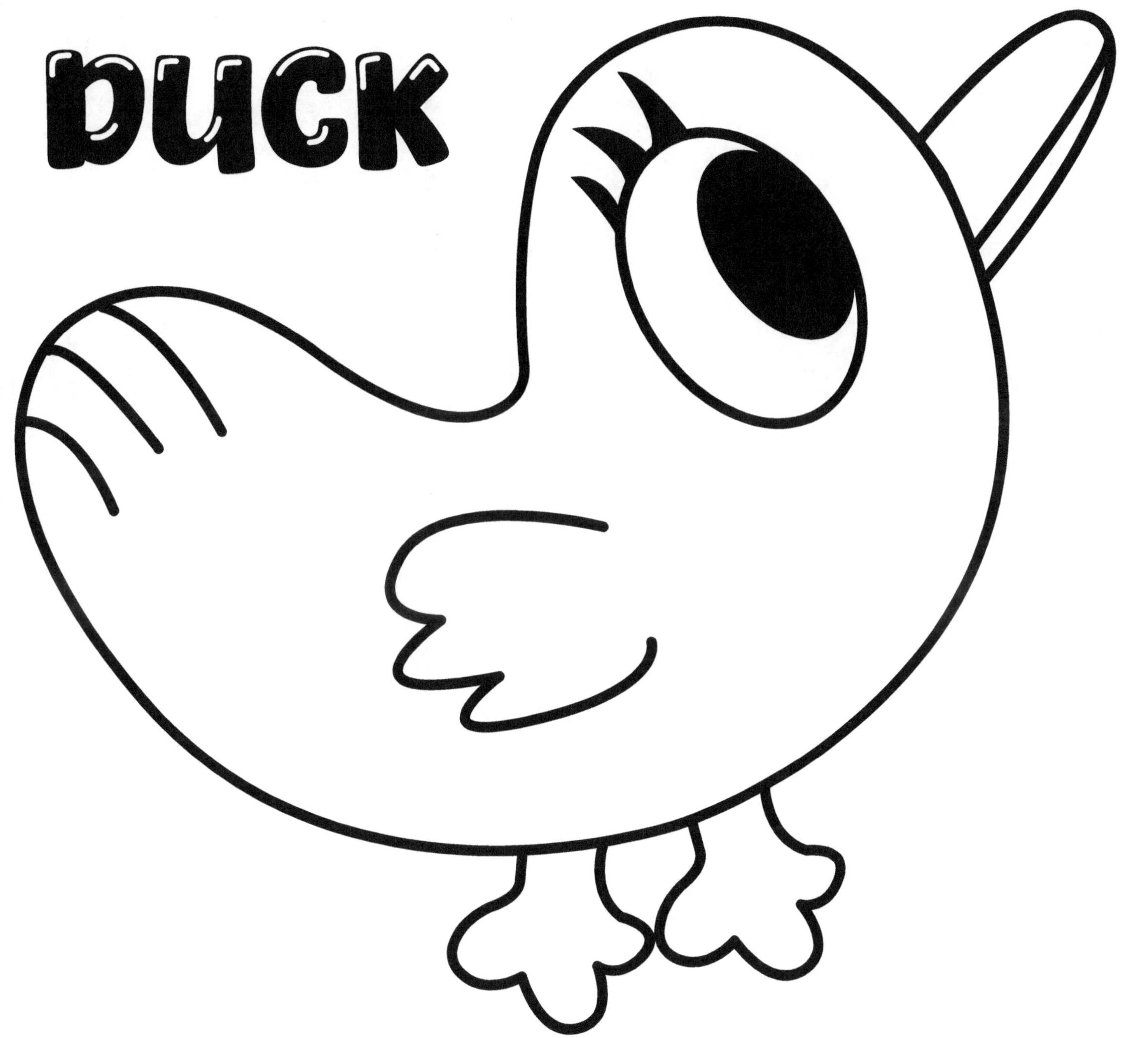
DUCK

BUTTERFLY

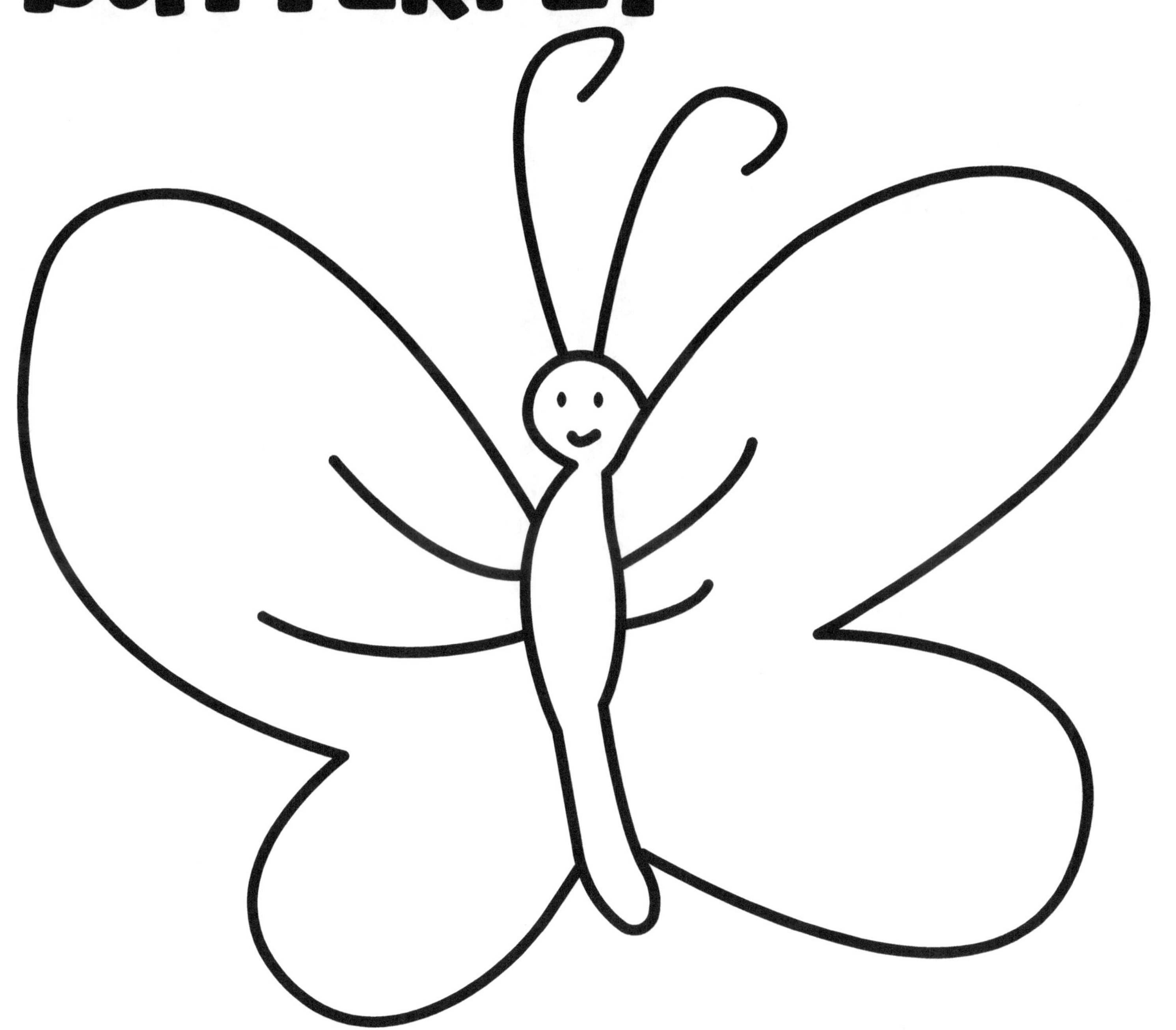

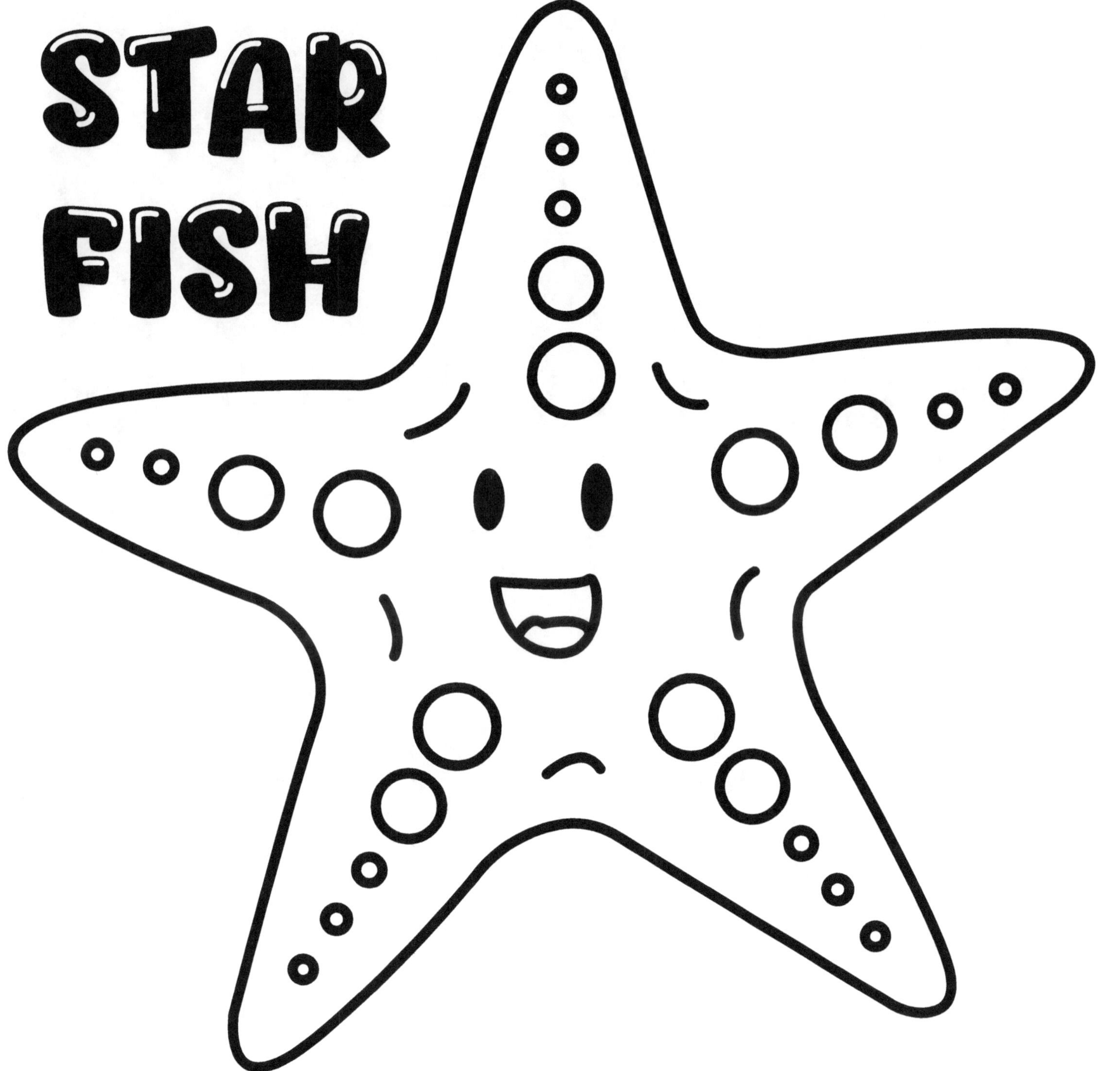

STAR
FISH

PARROT

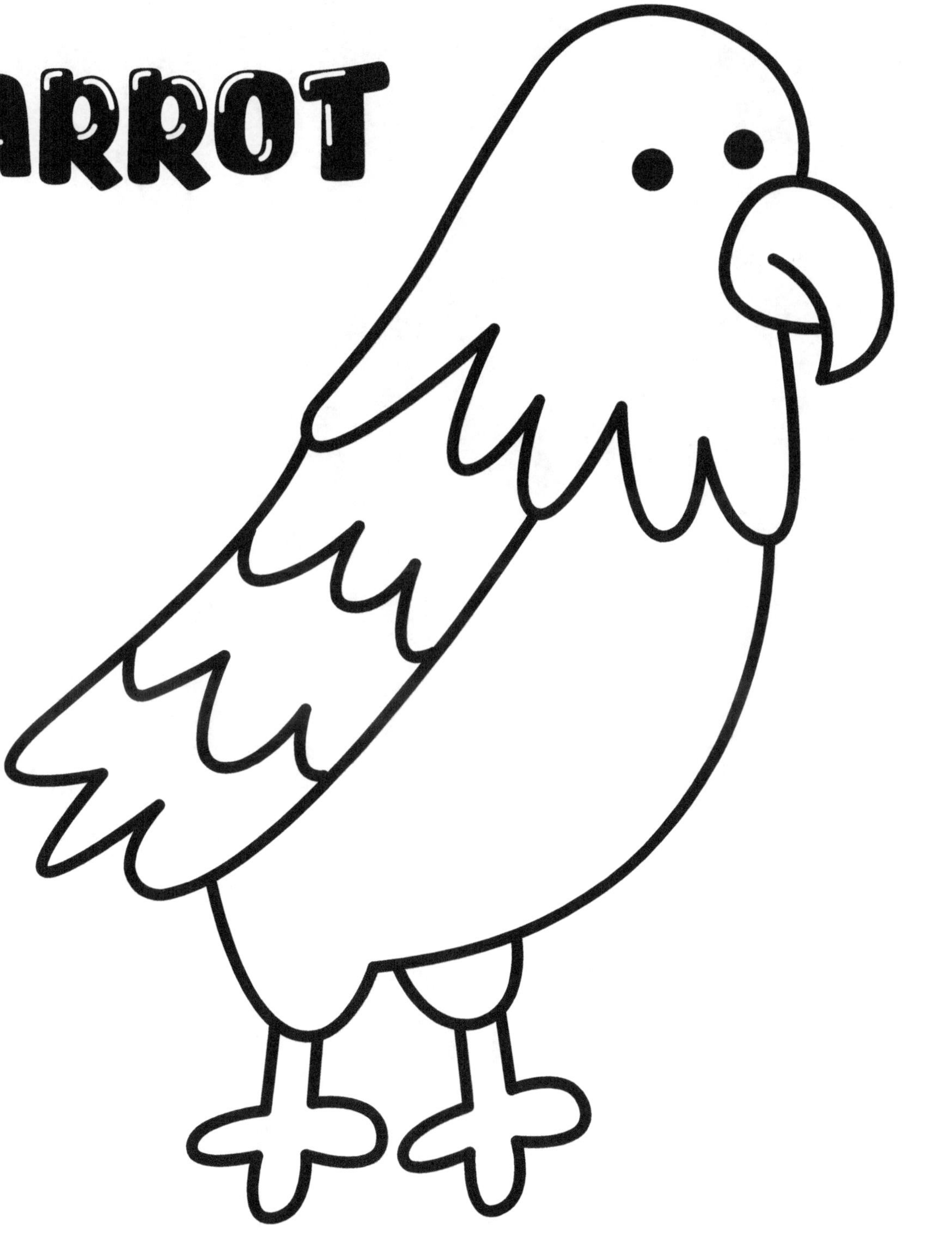

JELLY FISH

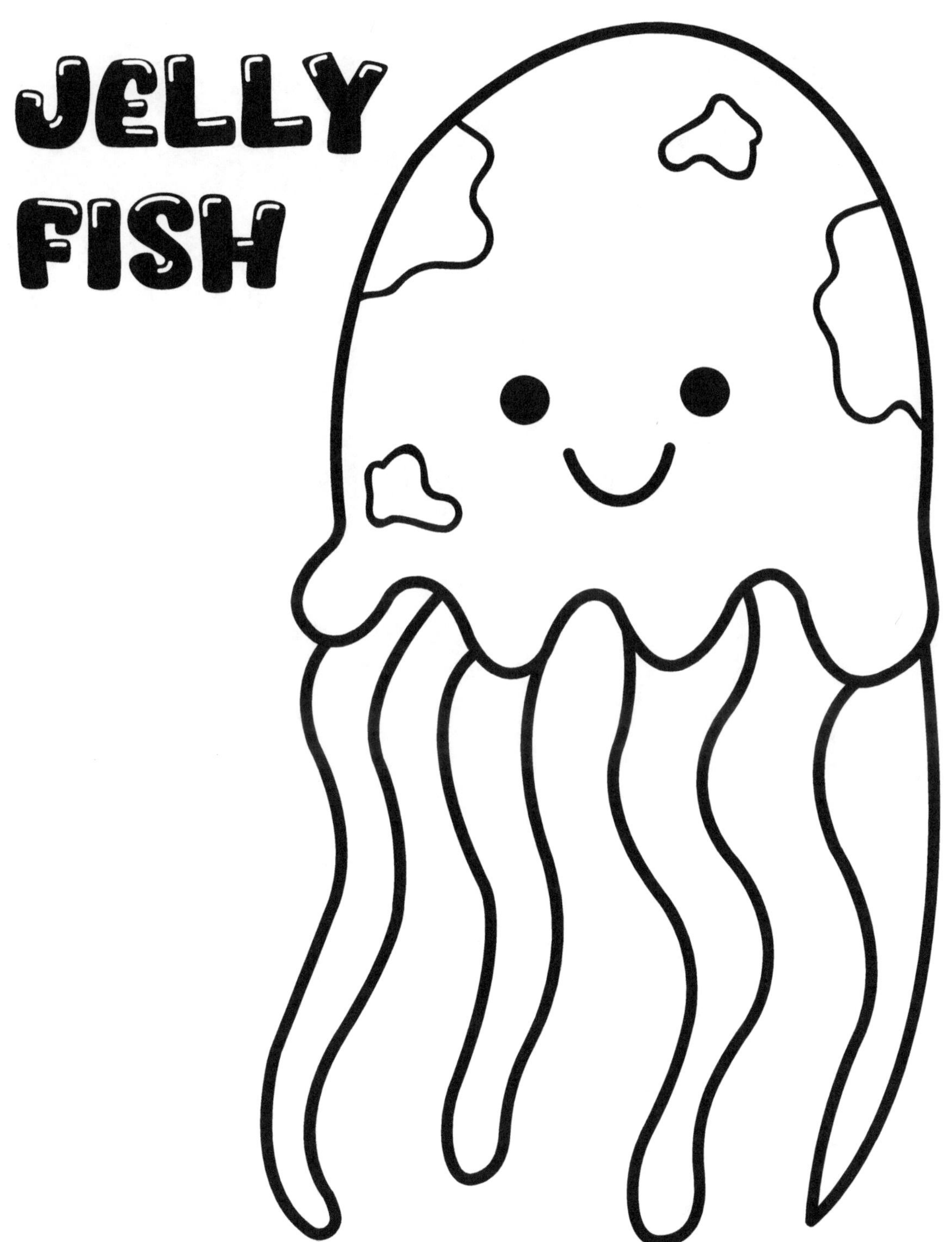

DOLPHIN

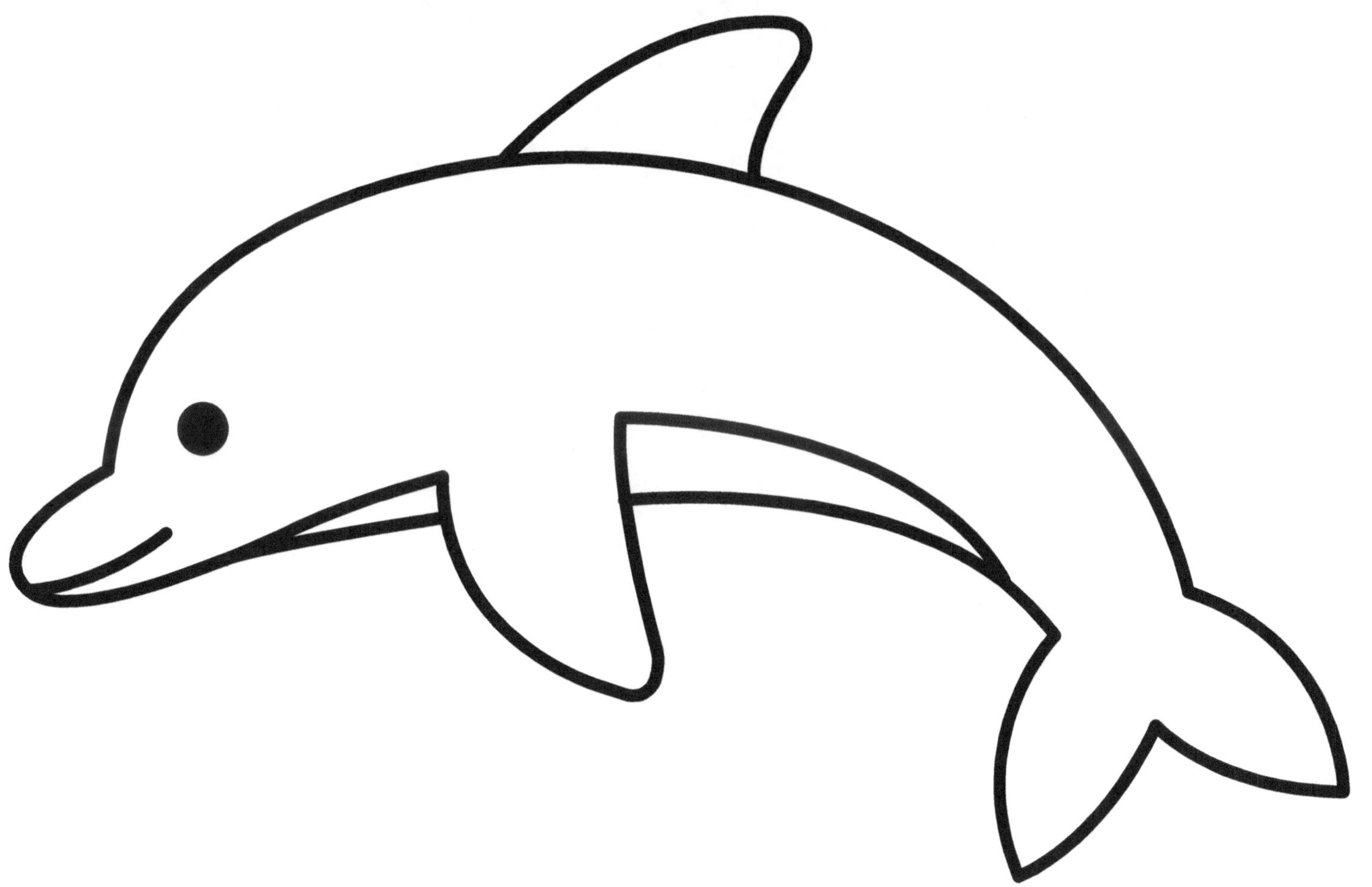

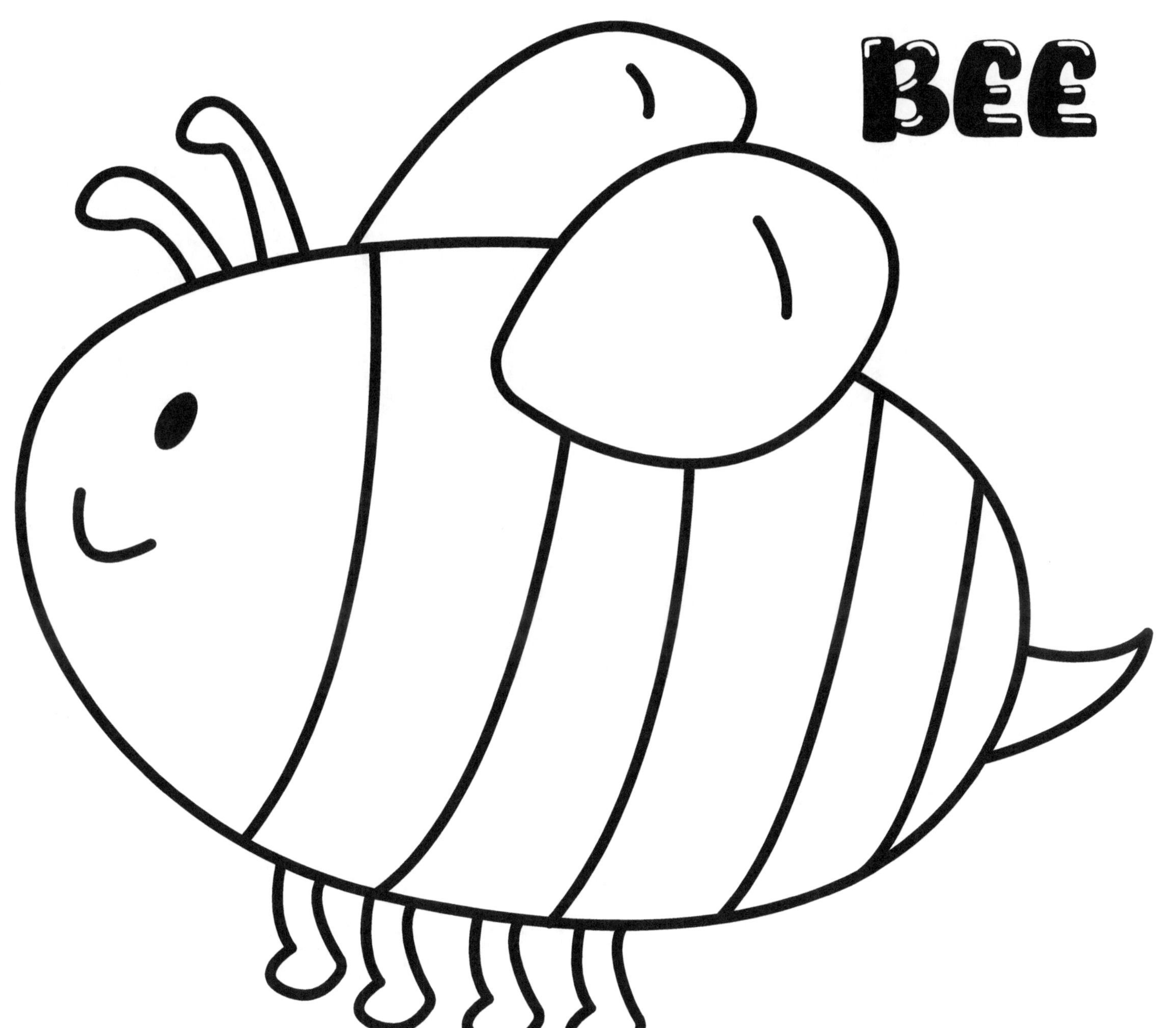
BEE

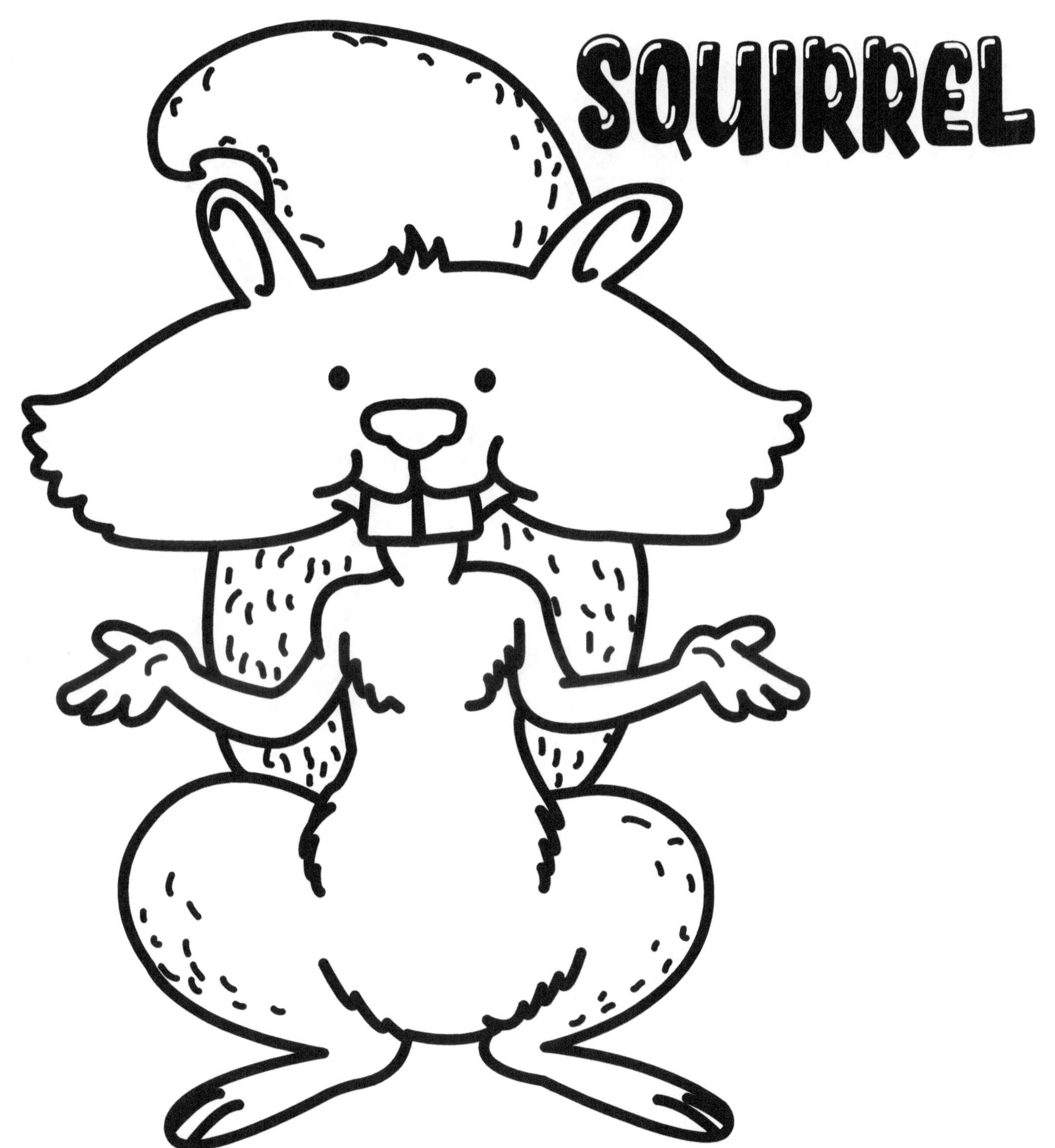

SQUIRREL

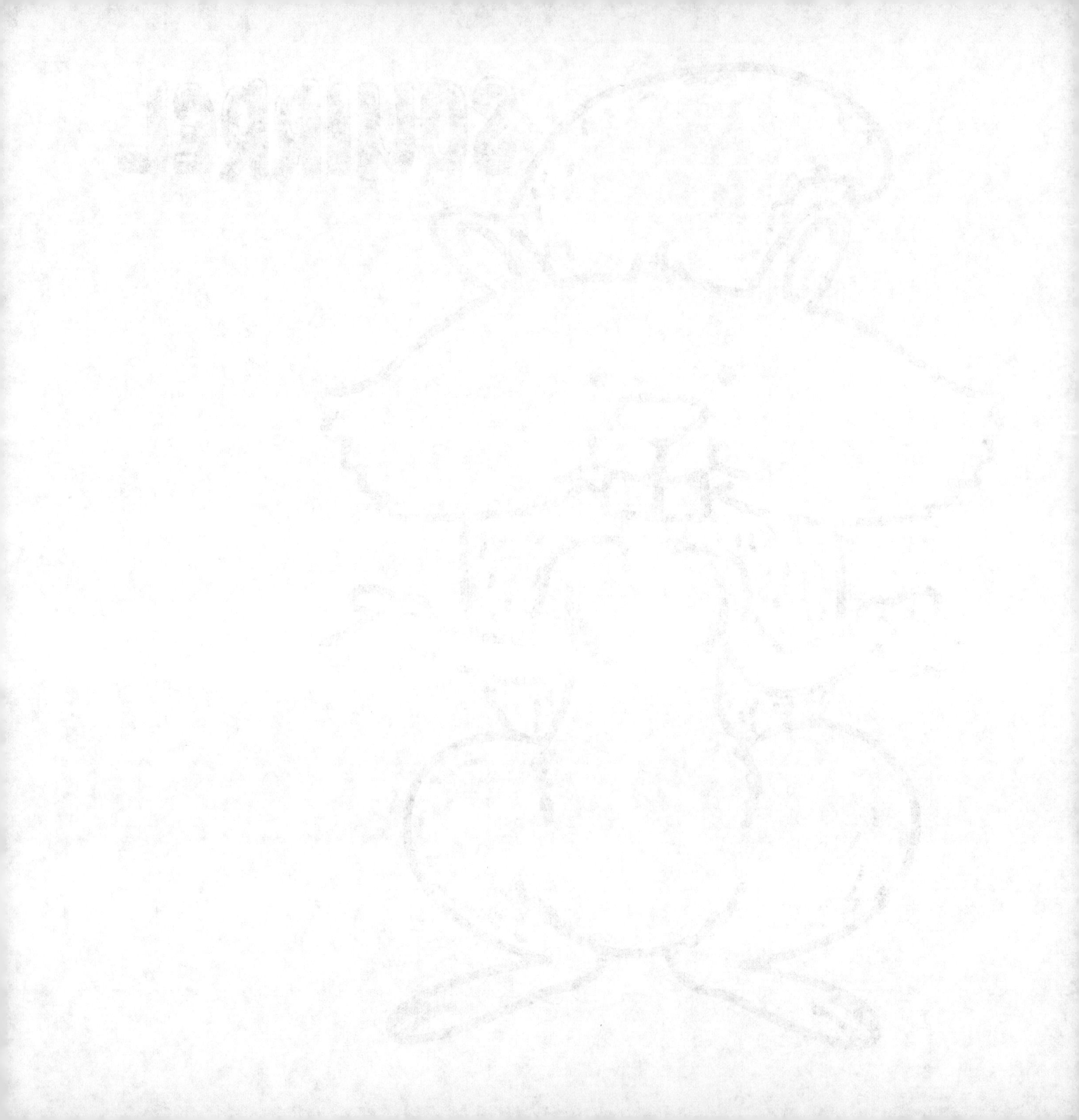

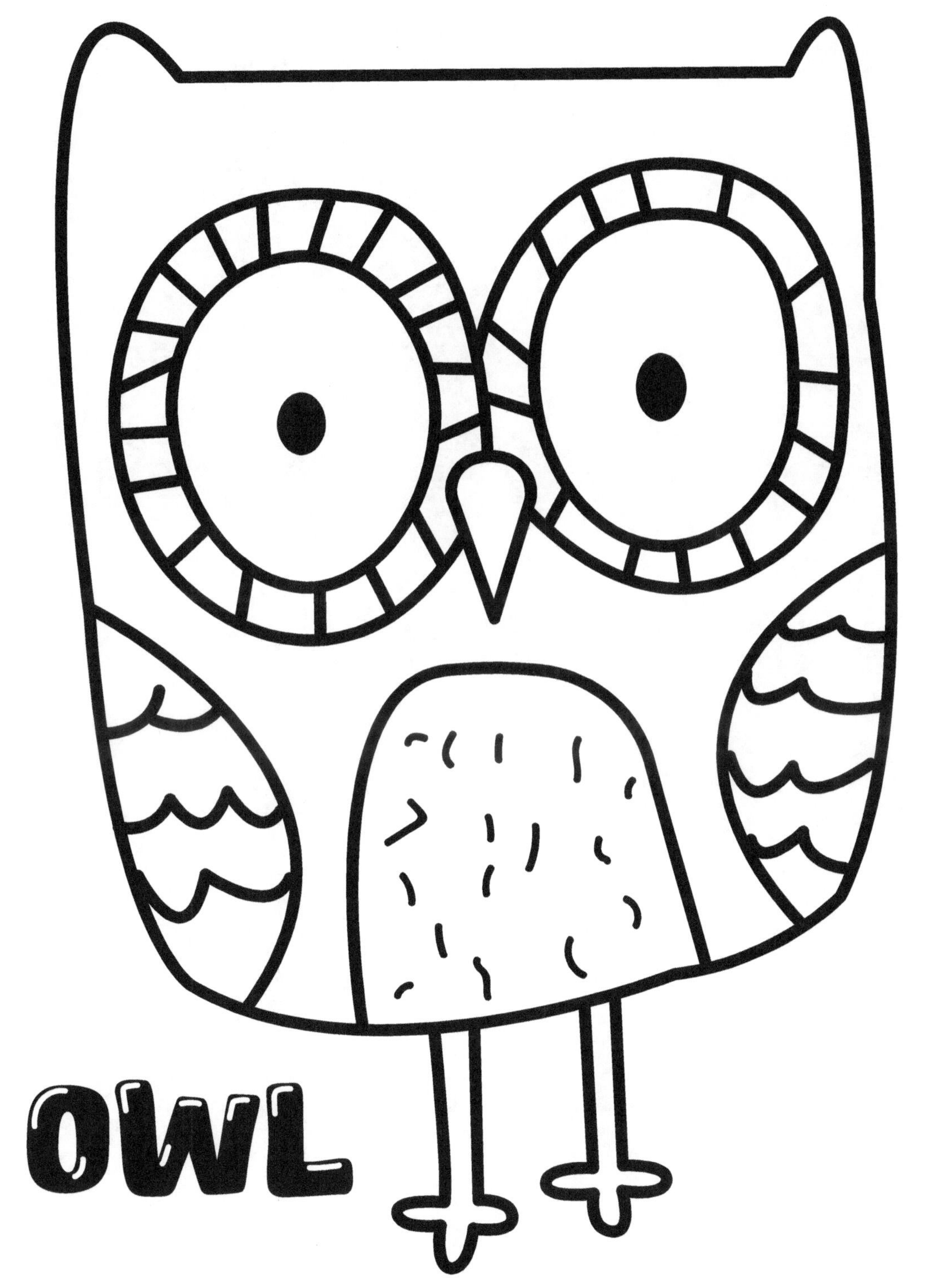

OWL

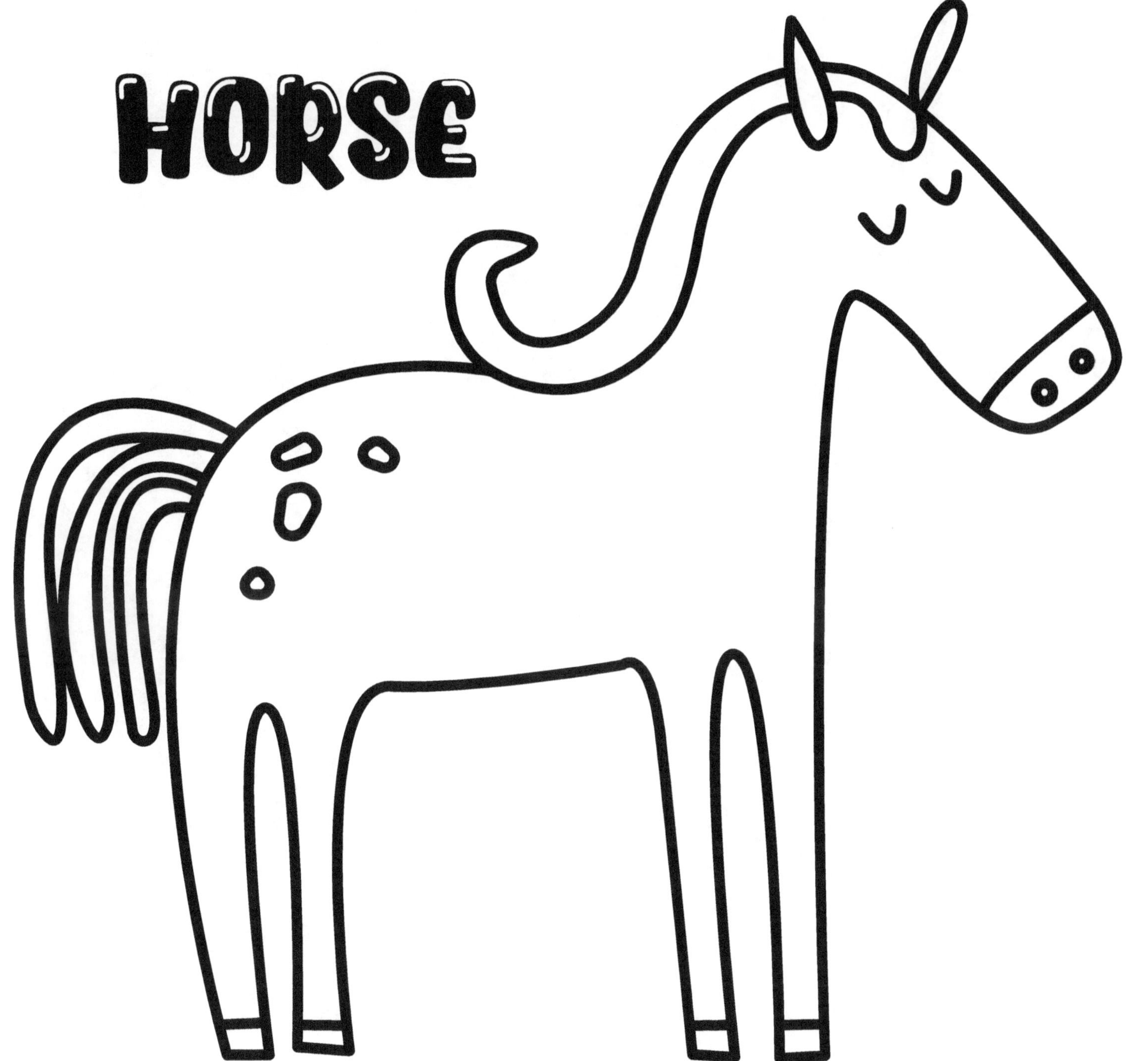

HORSE

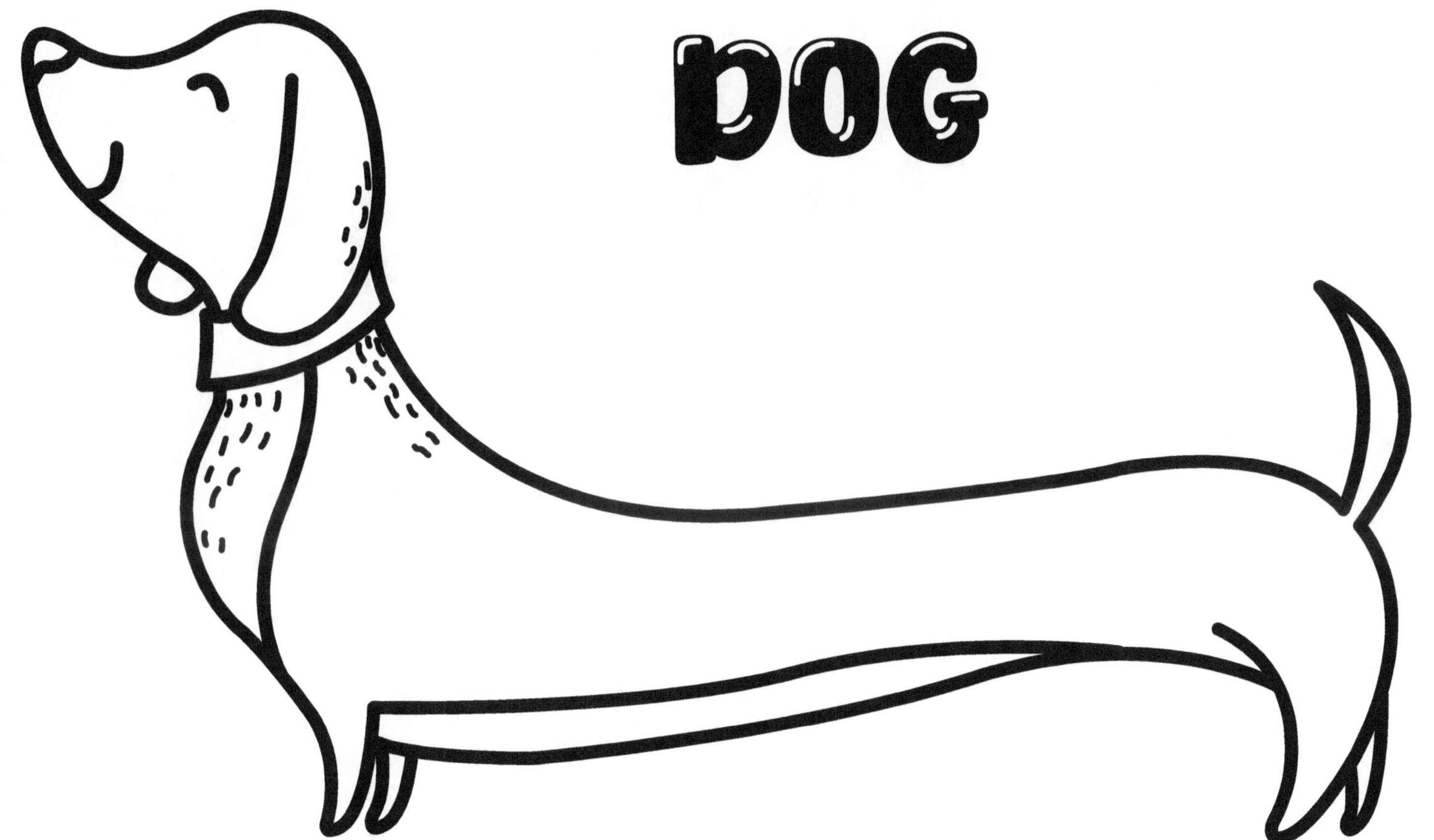
DOG

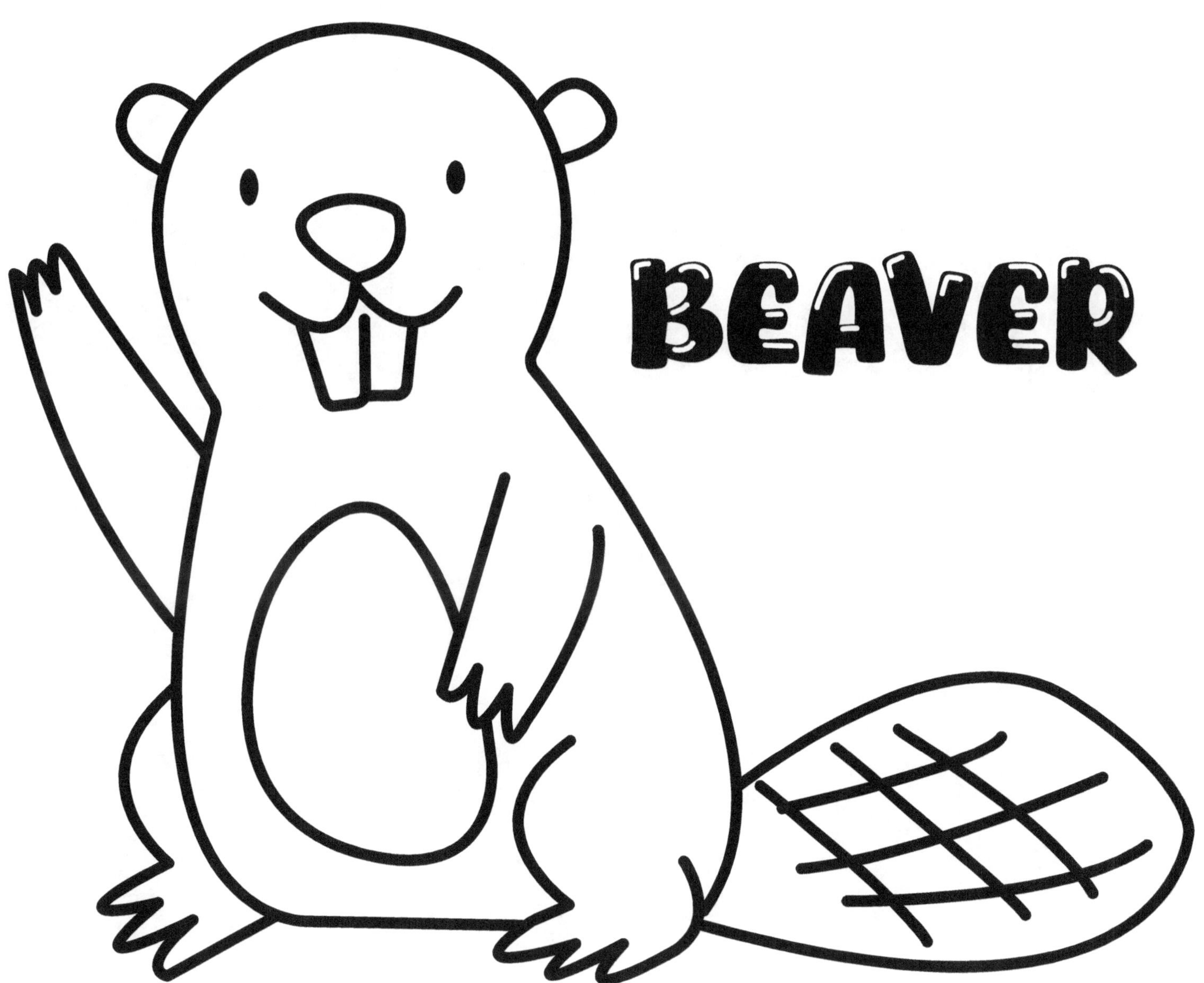
BEAVER

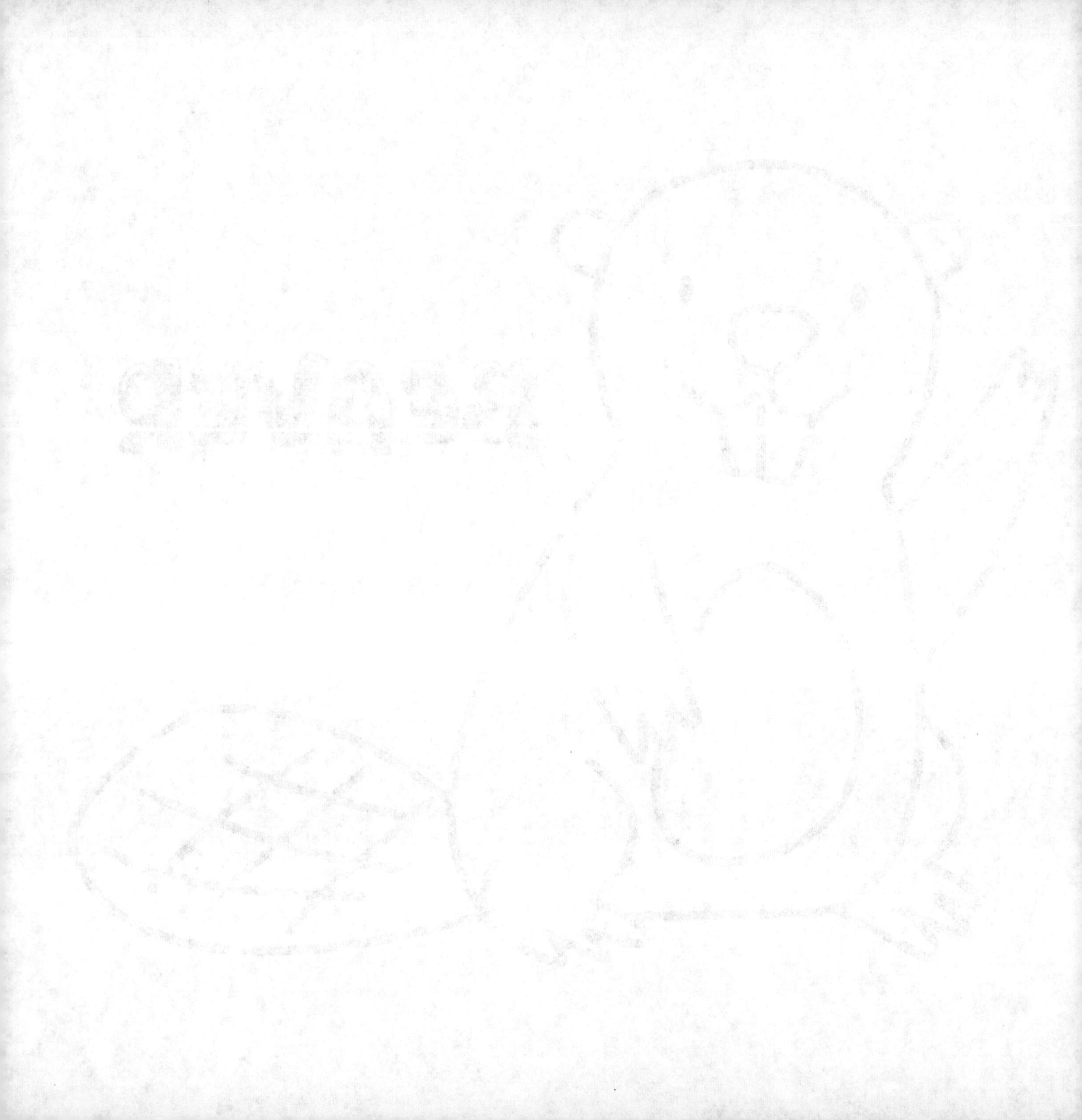

SNAIL

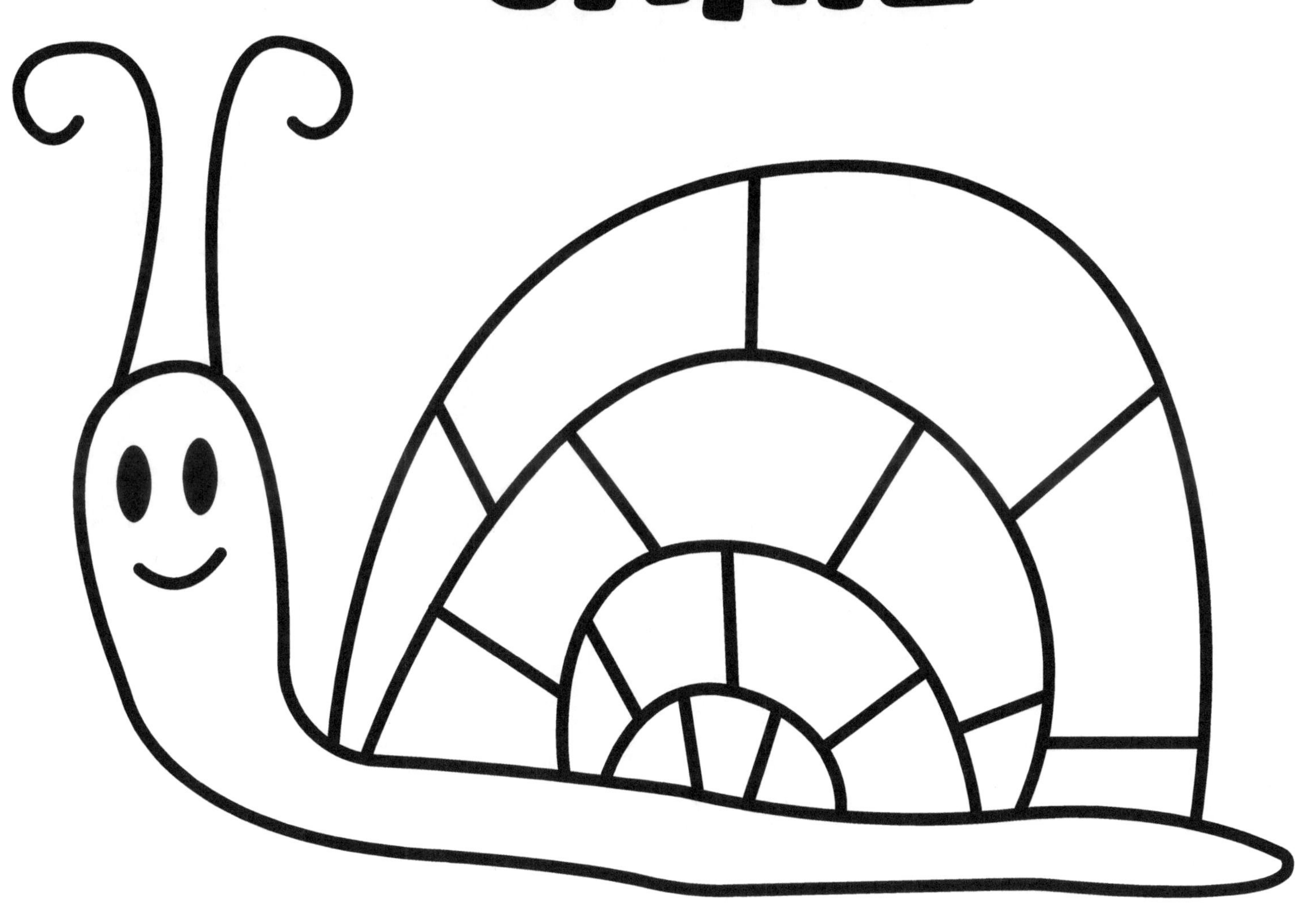

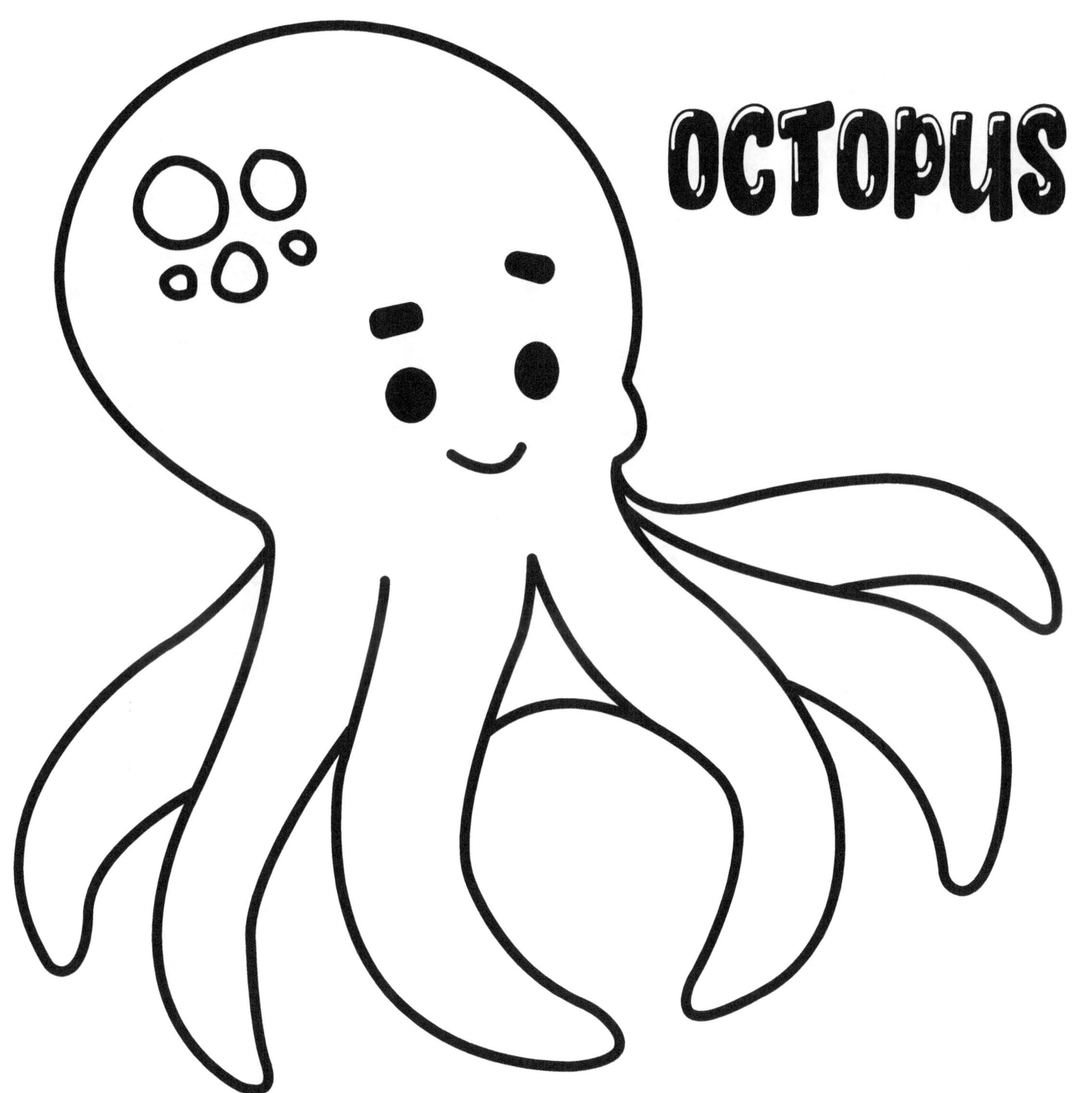
OCTOPUS

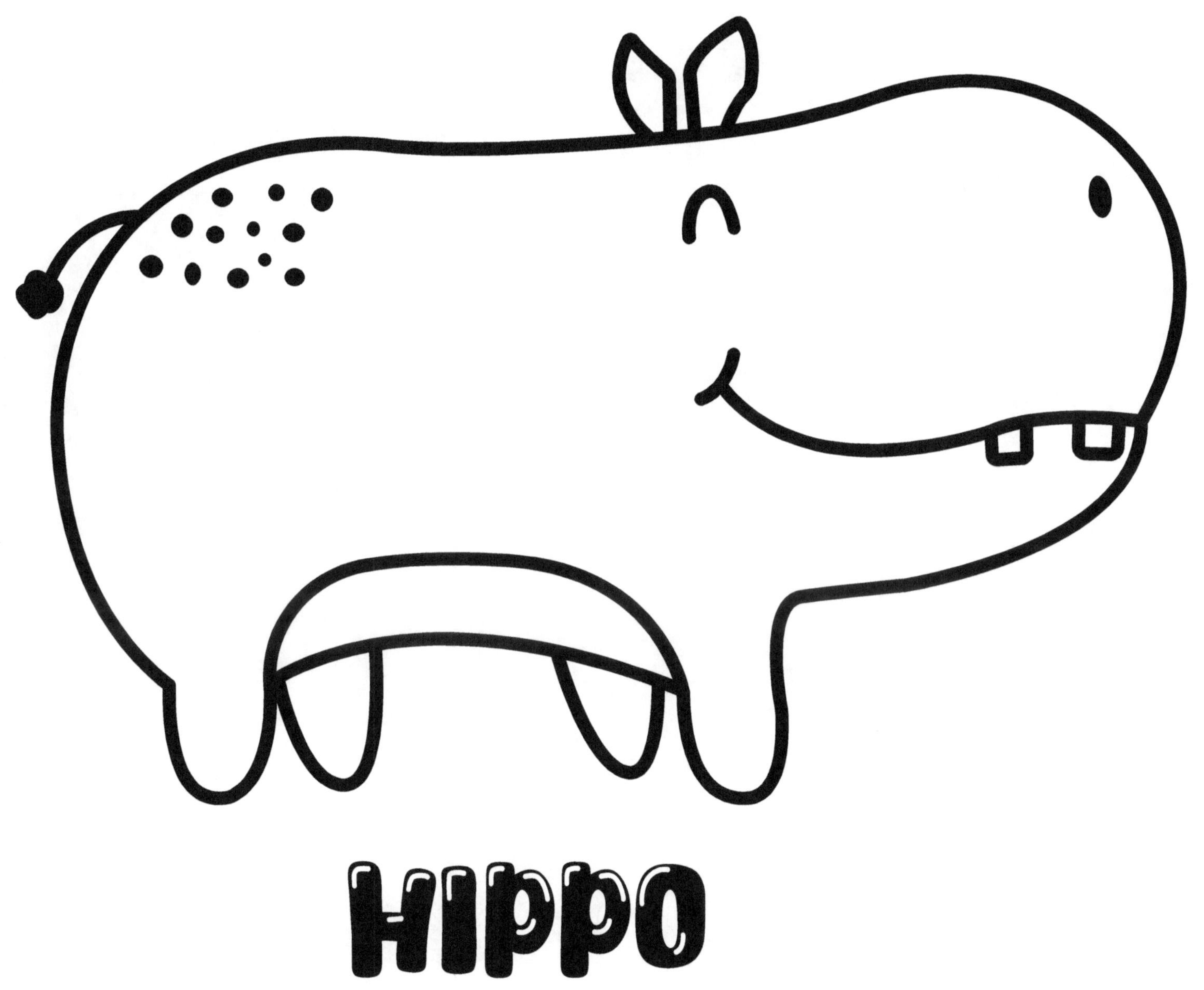
HIPPO

DEER

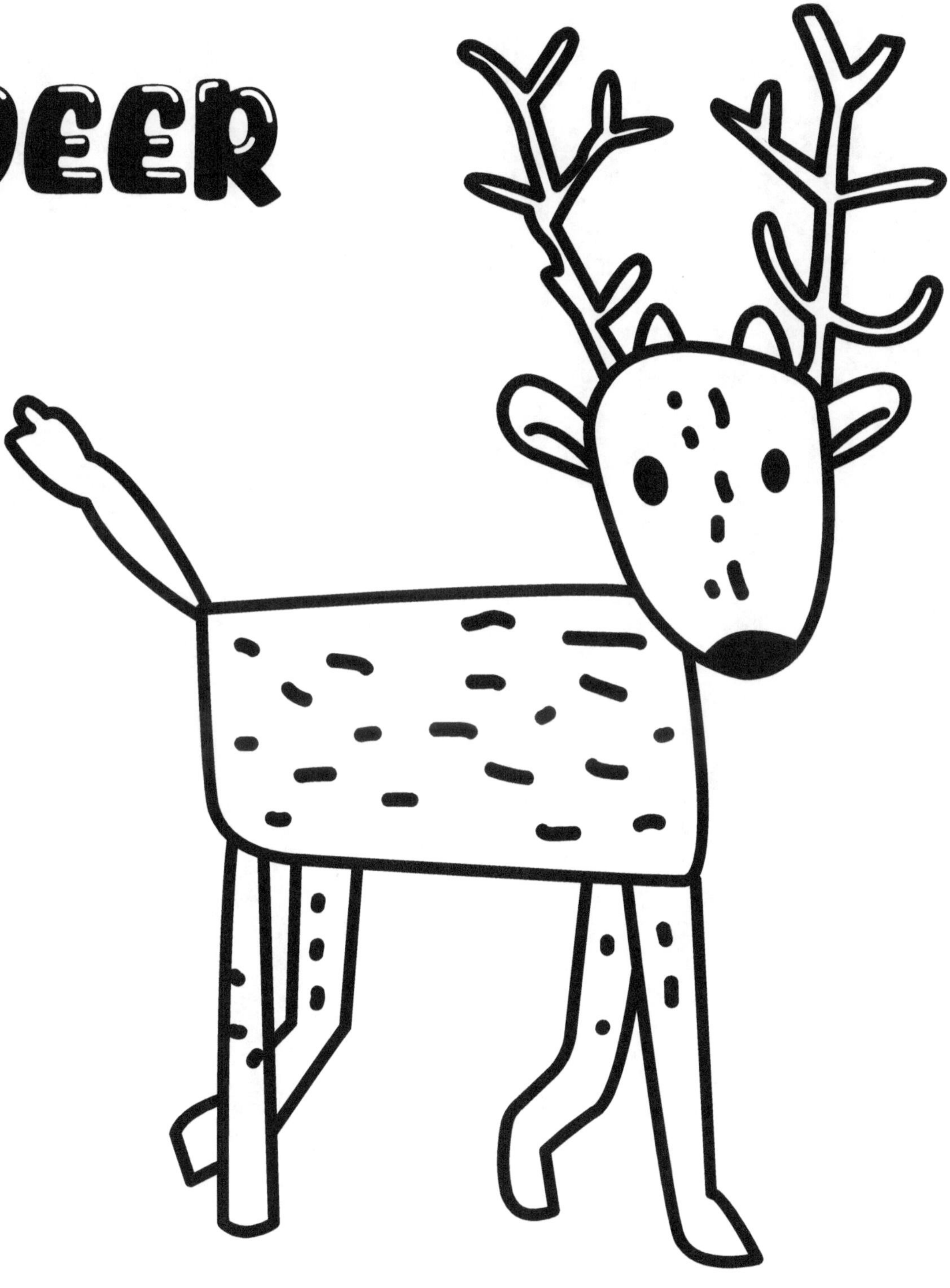

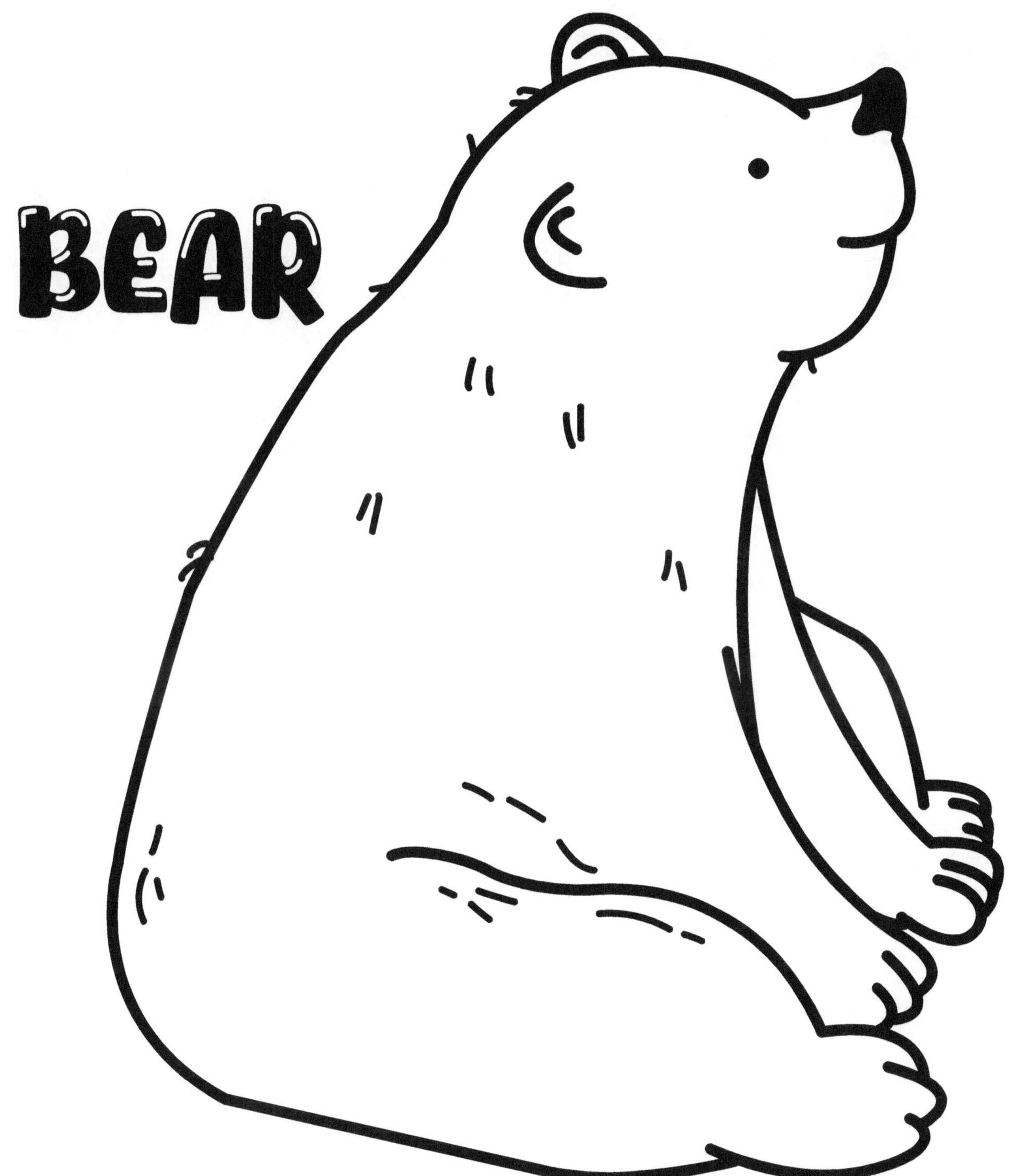

BEAR

WORM

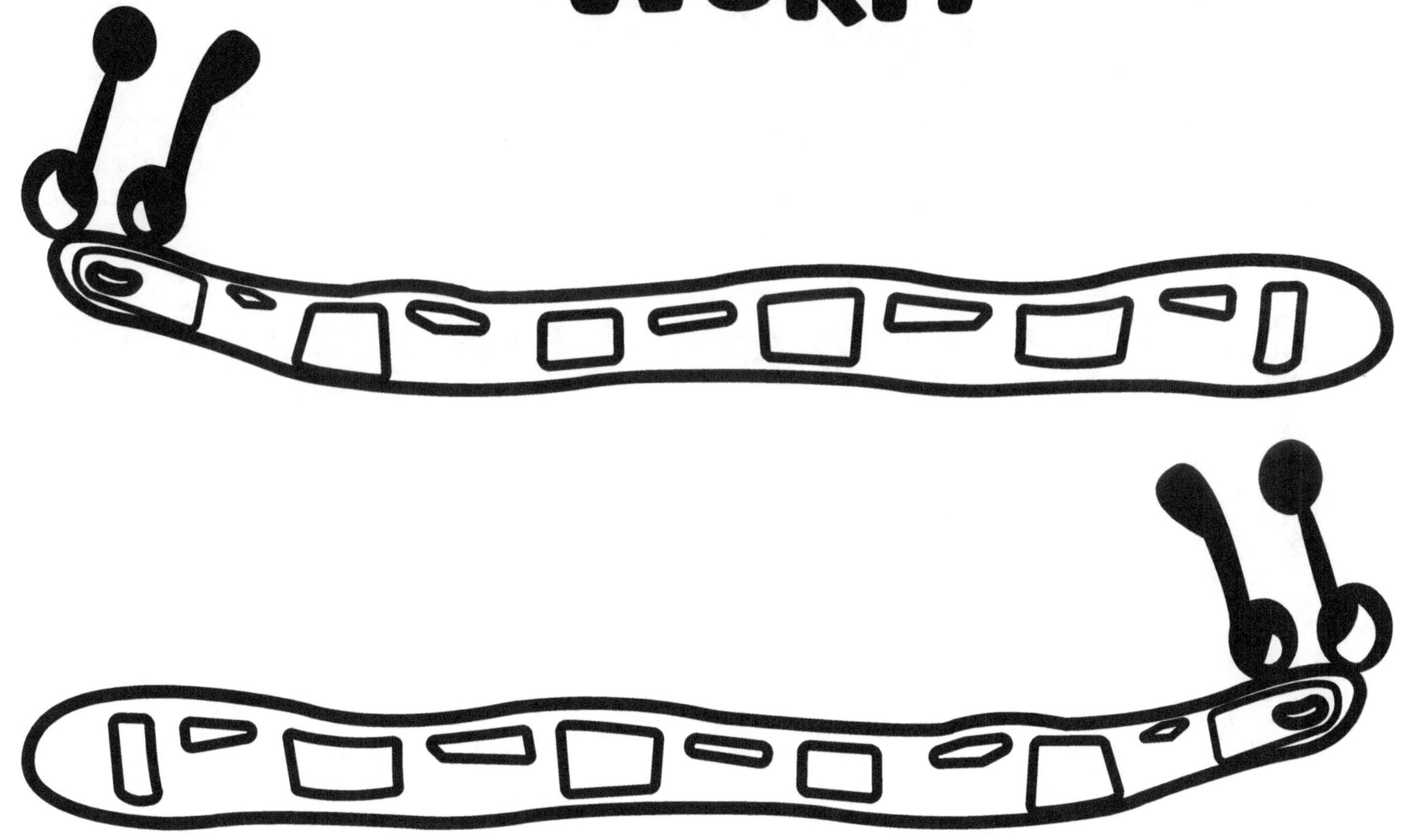

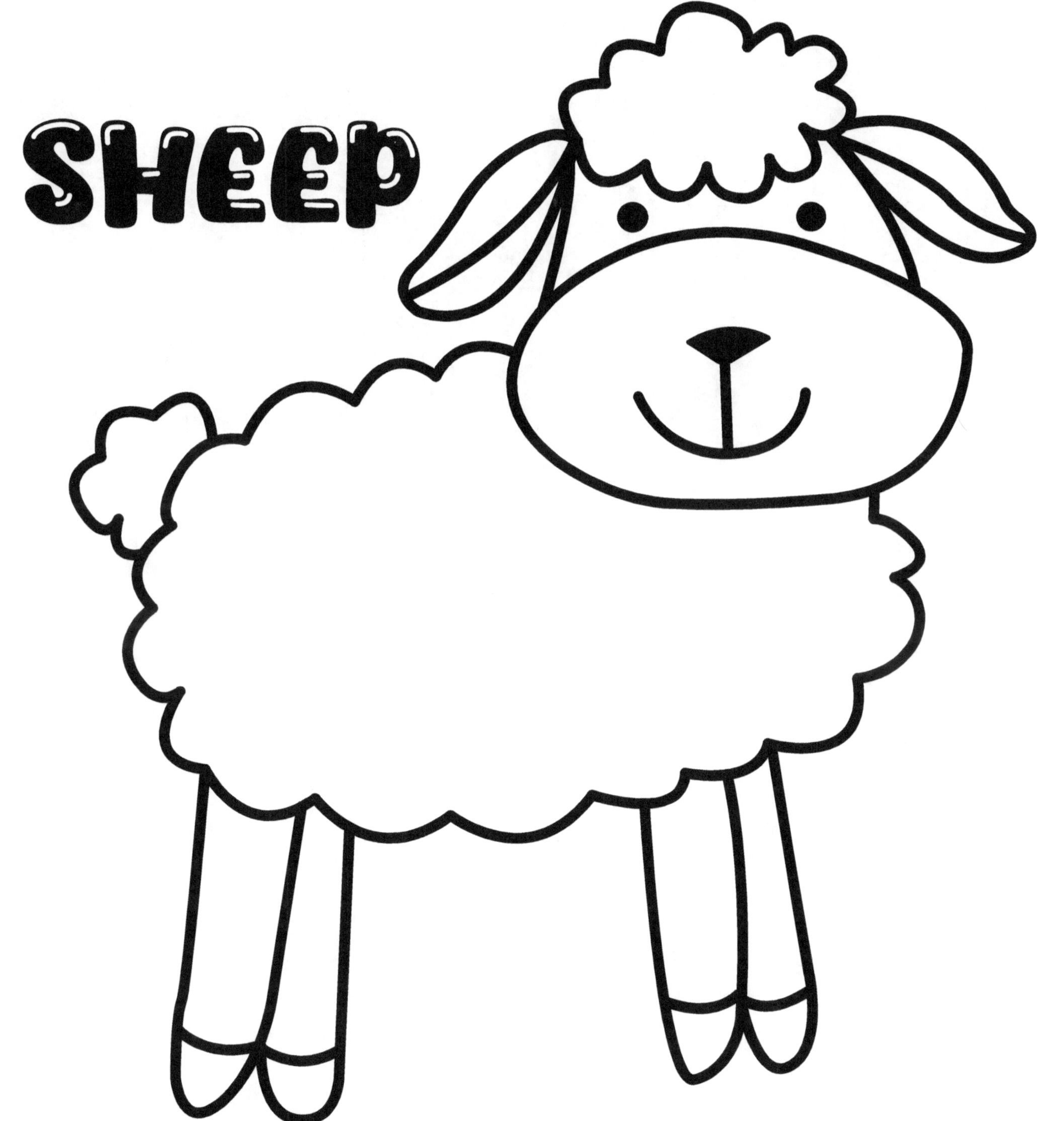
SHEEP

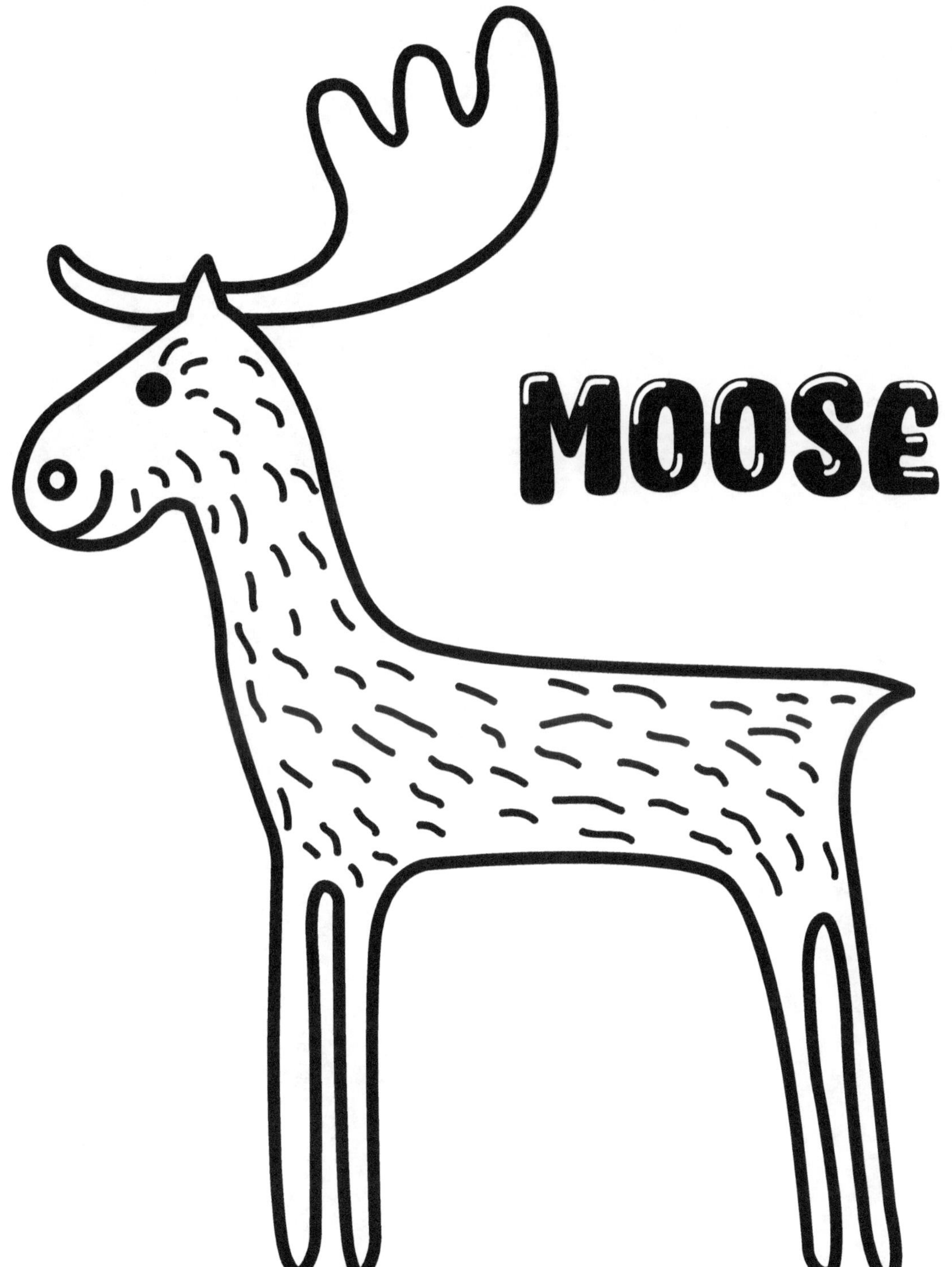

MOOSE

GOAT

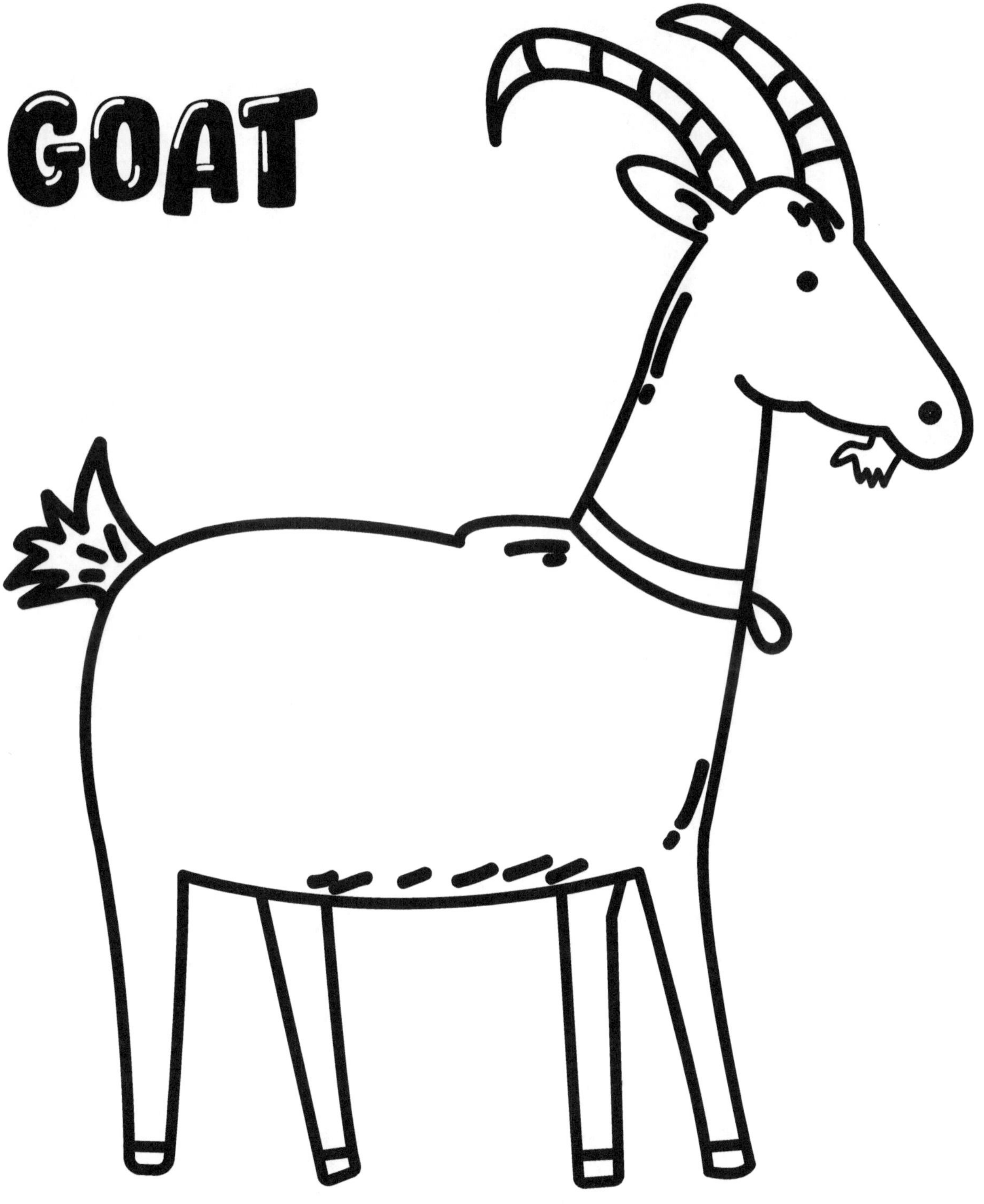

CROCODILE

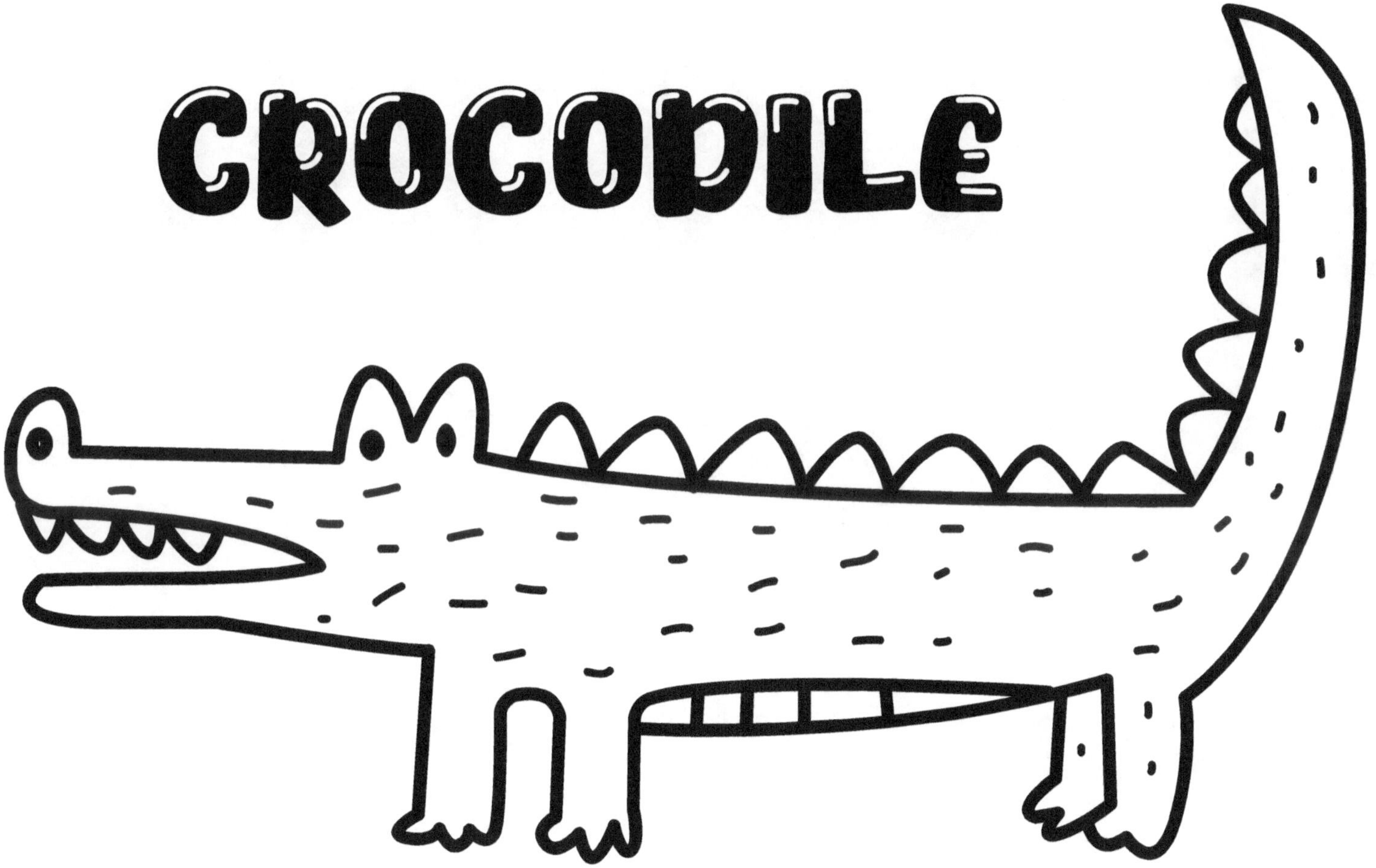